W9-AWL-140

COUNTING SHEEP

Also by Art Buchwald:

THE ESTABLISHMENT IS ALIVE AND WELL
IN WASHINGTON

HAVE I EVER LIED TO YOU?

SON OF THE GREAT SOCIETY

AND THEN I TOLD THE PRESIDENT

I CHOSE CAPITOL PUNISHMENT

IS IT SAFE TO DRINK THE WATER?

HOW MUCH IS THAT IN DOLLARS?

DON'T FORGET TO WRITE

MORE CAVIAR

BRAVE COWARD

ART BUCHWALD'S PARIS

A GIFT FROM THE BOYS   (novel)

PARIS AFTER DARK   (guide)

ART BUCHWALD'S SECRET LIST TO PARIS   (guide)

ART
BUCHWALD

COUNTING
SHEEP

THE LOG AND THE COMPLETE PLAY

Sheep on the Runway

G. P. Putnam's Sons, New York

Copyright © 1969, 1970 by Art Buchwald

All rights reserved. This book, or parts thereof, must
not be reproduced in any form without permission.
Published simultaneously in Canada
by Longmans Canada Limited, Toronto.

Library of Congress Catalog Card Number: 79-127713

PRINTED IN THE UNITED STATES OF AMERICA

This play is the sole property of the author and is fully protected
by copyright. It may not be acted by professionals or by amateurs
without written consent. Public readings and radio or television
broadcasts are likewise forbidden. All inquiries concerning rights
should be addressed to the author's agent, the William Morris
Agency, 1350 Avenue of the Americas, New York, New York 10019.

To Roger Stevens, Robert Whitehead
Gene Saks, and Joe Stein

THE LOG

1. In the Beginning

A Column Written on January 12, 1969

Power, the opiate of the people who live in Washington, is starting to slip through the hands of the old administration and is being grabbed by the new. There are signs of the switch taking place every day. For example, Tuesday I was at the Sans Souci Restaurant, the place where the White House power structure usually has lunch.

One of President Johnson's aides came in and was escorted to his usual table. He sat there for two hours, alone. The person he was supposed to have lunch with never showed up.

The man I was with, who has lived through several administration changeovers in Washington, shook his head sadly and said, "The poor SOB. They're trying to tell him something."

"Is that how they usually do it?" I asked.

"Sometimes they cancel his table before he arrives. That way nobody knows he was stood up for lunch. This way everybody knows. It will be all over town in an hour."

"But suppose the person who was supposed to have lunch with him just couldn't make it?"

"You don't understand. If you've got the power, the person *makes* it. Somebody else gets stood up. But if you don't have the power anymore, then you get stood up.

"Look, he's looking over here and smiling at us. Whatever you do, don't smile back."

"But he's my friend," I protested. "If he smiles at me, I'll have to smile back."

"He doesn't want you just to smile back. He wants you to invite him to sit with us, so it doesn't look as if he's been stood up. We can't afford that."

"Why not?"

"You don't know anything about this town, do you? Suppose word got out that we had lunch with him—I mean just two weeks before inauguration."

"Well, heck, he's still a decent guy, even if he is on his way out."

"That's not the point, stupid," my friend said. "We have to deal with the new guys over at the White House, and if they think we have any ties with the old guys, they won't trust us. If you still want to have something to do with that loser, meet him at a Howard Johnson's, but don't get me involved. I've got my job to think of."

"Are you trying to tell me that the new guys wouldn't trust us if we bought an old administration guy a cup of coffee?"

"I'm trying to tell you that everyone in this restaurant is aware of what is going on. Sure, it would be a nice, brave, gutty thing to wave and say, 'Come on over for a brandy.' And there are probably a few people in the restaurant who would admire us for it. But a majority of the people in this restaurant feel exactly as I do. The guy came in here alone. Let him leave alone."

"It seems so cruel."

"Government is cruel," my friend said. "But he will be all right. He'll probably get a hundred thousand dollars a year when he gets out of the White House, not to mention a half-million-dollar advance on a book, plus lecture fees. He's not going to starve to death."

"But the thought of nobody ever eating lunch with him again," I said. "Couldn't I just go over to his table and say good-bye?" I asked.

"I wouldn't chance it. Herb Klein just came in." My friend waved wildly at Klein, Mr. Nixon's new communications chief. "Hiya, Herb, baby. How's the old boy!"

My friend muttered to me, "Wave at him. Maybe he'll stop by the table for a minute. It won't hurt us if he does."

In the excitement, my friend from the White House got up from the table and left the restaurant. Not one person in the Sans Souci noticed he was gone.

The preceding column which I wrote just before President Nixon's inauguration had a ring of truth to it. The man I was talking about was Roger L. Stevens, who was at the time the chairman of the National Council on the Arts and special assistant to the President during the Johnson and Kennedy years.

Stevens, a glutton for thankless causes, was also chairman of the Board of Trustees of the John F. Kennedy Center for the Performing Arts. Before going to work for the government, he made a fortune in real estate and at one time bought the Empire State Building with a few close friends. But his real love was the theater. He produced or co-produced 125 Broadway shows, including

13

West Side Story, The Best Man, Mary, Mary, The Bad Seed, Tea and Sympathy, and *Sabrina Fair.*

The only time I ever saw him was at the Sans Souci, where we kept bumping into each other at lunch. Every time I met him he said, "Why don't you write a play for me to produce?" and I always replied, "Yeah, sure."

Writing plays is pretty tough in Washington. Writing about anything except politics is pretty tough. Once Russell Baker, the resident humorist at the New York *Times,* and I collaborated on a treatment for a movie. It was about Khrushchev's nephew, who was sent to the United States to be a spy and wound up joining the John Birch Society.

The movie producers said it was "too implausible," so Baker and I decided to forget it. You can imagine how mad we were when Joseph Stalin's daughter came to the United States a year later and joined the Book-of-the-Month Club.

One day a few months after Nixon was sworn in, Stevens was booted, unceremoniously, out of his job at the Arts Council by some lackey at the White House. The aide announced it to the press without bothering to tell Stevens first. When the Nixon people realized what a good job Stevens had done, he was asked to stay. But it was too late. He decided he wanted out.

The next time I met Stevens at the Sans Souci he said, "All right, I'm out of the government now. How about that play you promised to write for me?"

"Yeah, sure," I said.

"Let's have lunch tomorrow and talk about it."

"Yeah, sure," I said, trying to figure how I was going to get out of this one.

The next day at lunch he said, "Now tell me your idea for a play."

I didn't want to look like someone who didn't even have an idea for a play, so I started winging it. "I have this idea about a political columnist who not only reports news, but makes it. He visits an embassy in the Himalayas where the ambassador, a political appointee, is stationed. The ambassador feels he should have gotten London or Paris for all the money he gave the party. But the columnist tells him not to worry."

"What else?" Roger asked.

"That's it," I said, thinking that was the end of it.

But Roger was not to be discouraged. "Okay, write it."

"You're serious?" I asked.

"Give me the draft of the first act, and if I like it, I'll put up my own money."

I thought of all the playwrights in the country with plays already written trying to find a producer, and here, just because I was trying to please a guy who was buying me lunch, I had everything I needed, except a play.

I was certain he would forget about it, as I intended to do.

A week later Stevens called and asked how I was doing.

"Great," I said. "Just great."

"When can I see something?" he wanted to know.

"In a few weeks."

I hung up and said to my wife, "You know, he was serious about my writing a play."

"You should have paid for the lunch," she said. "Then you wouldn't owe him anything."

"You know, if we hit, we could make a lot of money."

"Just make sure they pay your expenses if they make you go to New York."

"I read an article which said that Neil Simon makes fifteen thousand dollars a week."

"Don't let them make you take the shuttle. Tell them you insist on flying first class. They'll have more respect for you."

I went into the library, stuck a sheet of paper in the typewriter, and started tapping "ACT ONE—SCENE ONE—An Embassy in Nonomura———."

A few weeks later I took three scenes over to Stevens' house in Georgetown and left them there. He called me a day later.

"I like it," he said. "I'll sign a contract with you to produce it."

I held my hand over the phone and said to my wife, "He likes it. He wants to produce it."

"Ask him about the expenses to New York."

"Hey, Roger," I said. "Besides all the money I can make writing a hit play, who pays my expenses from Washington to New York?"

"I do," he said.

I hung up and looked at my wife. "We're in show biz."

This was not my first experience in the theater—not by a long shot. When I was going to USC in 1948, I wrote the book for a varsity show musical titled *No Love Atoll* with a roommate named Ray Pippin. It was about the atomic experiments at Bikini and had music, songs, and dances and ran for four days. The SC *Daily Trojan* gave us a rave review.

My second experience in the theater came in London when two English producers Wolf Mankowitz and Oscar Lewinstein bought the rights to my column for a review titled *The Art of Living*. It played at the Criterion at Piccadilly Circus for six months.

The third experience took place in 1967 when a young woman producer, Stephanie Sills, decided to do a musical review of my more recent columns. Everybody thought it was a great idea. Miss Sills had just produced *America Hurrah*, a very successful Off Broadway play, and her backers were dying to invest in her new venture.

The only problem was that there was no one to direct it. The first person we approached said he was very interested. But then he decided to go to alimony jail instead. The second person we asked also agreed to do it. But then he visited his astrologer, who warned him not to do it.

The final director, who said he'd be very happy to do it, never showed up for rehearsal.

So much for Off Broadway. It just didn't seem to be my turf.

I finished the first draft in about three weeks and went to New York in early July to meet with Roger Stevens and his partner, Robert Whitehead. Before the meeting I stopped off at Fifty-ninth Street and Madison Avenue to get a shine. Seated in the next chair was David Merrick, an old acquaintance.

Counting Sheep

MERRICK: What are you doing in New York?

ME: I just wrote a play and came to talk to my producers Stevens and Whitehead.

MERRICK: Why didn't you show it to me first?

ME: Because they asked me to write it.

MERRICK (*angry*): You mean just because someone asks you to write a play, you sit down and write one?

ME: That's the size of it.

MERRICK: Why didn't I ask you to write a play?

ME: Beats the hell out of me.

MERRICK: Is the contract signed yet?

ME: Yup.

MERRICK: Well, for your sake I hope it's a success. For my sake I hope it isn't.

ME: I thought everything successful on Broadway helps everything else.

MERRICK: That's a bunch of crap. The only hits I root for are my own. Give Roger and Bob my best.

LUNCH AT THE CARLTON HOUSE IN NEW YORK

Roger Stevens, Bob Whitehead, and myself. Bob Whitehead is the creative member of the production company. His hits have included *A Man for All Seasons, The Member of the Wedding, Waltz of the Toreadors, The Visit, The Price,* and *The Prime of Miss Jean Brodie.*

WHITEHEAD: I like your play very much.

ME: That's great.

WHITEHEAD: It's very funny.

ME: Thank you.

WHITEHEAD: And it says something.

18

ME: I was hoping it would.

WHITEHEAD: Now let's get serious.

ME: How's that?

WHITEHEAD: It has to be completely rewritten.

ME: I was afraid you'd say that.

If I agree to write, Roger and Bob will start a search for a director. Good news. We can have Mike Nichols if we wait until March 6, 1995.

Other names come to mind: Joe Hardy, Joe Anthony, Joe Layton, Joe Ferrer. It's hard to find someone in the theater who isn't named Joe. We settle for a Gene— Gene Saks, who is a first-class actor turned director. He directed *Enter Laughing, Nobody Loves an Albatross, Generation, Half a Sixpence, Mame,* and the movies *Barefoot in the Park, The Odd Couple,* and *Cactus Flower.* Saks has a beard and bushy eyebrows. He came to see me in Martha's Vineyard in August.

SAKS: They want me to direct your play.

ME: Great.

SAKS: I like it very much.

ME: Thank you.

SAKS: It's terribly funny.

ME: But. . . .

SAKS: But what?

ME: It has to be completely rewritten.

SAKS: How did you know I was going to say that?

ME: I just felt it.

Martha's Vineyard
August, 1969

I am working in a rented house in Vineyard Haven on Martha's Vineyard. It is owned by a dentist. His offices

19

are next to the room I have chosen to do my work. It is not the best condition to write a comedy.

I write "Enter Joe—Ah, Raymond, so glad to see you."

Sound of dentist's drill—"*zzzzzzz*"

"Raymond—Joe, you old son of a gun. It's great to see you."

"Please spit out."

"Joe—What a wonderful sunset."

"This won't hurt Mrs. Brustein. Trust me."

"Raymond—You don't get sunsets like that back in the States."

"Aghaghaghaghaghaghahgh . . . aghghgachacgh!!!!"

"Spit out, please."

"Joe—Ah, Martha, you look beautiful."

"Mrs. Brustein, just one more time. Please be brave."

"ZZZzzzzZZZzzz"

"Owowowowowowowowowowowowowwowowowowow!!!!"

"There, I told you it wouldn't hurt."

"Martha—Tell me, Joe, what are the people in America thinking?"

"Spit out, Mrs. Brustein. Thank you very much."

WHAT'S IN A NAME? SEPTEMBER, 1969

Title of the play has been changed many times. The original was *The Doves, the Hawks, and the Chickens.* Then it became *Broken Window.* This title was based on a brilliant theatrical idea of mine which would show a large picture window in the back of the stage which would break every time something happened outside the embassy. The story of our American policy would be told through the window.

20

They all thought the idea was great until they threw it out. It's impossible, they explained, to have a window in the back of the stage where everything happens, as the audience can't see it. Therefore, it's decided to have an imaginary window front stage center, and instead of *seeing* the glass break, we'd *hear* it. This also turned out to be a bad idea so we settled for having the picture window in the dining room, where it plays a very little part in the play.

I come up with a new title: *How to Fold the American Flag.* The idea for this title came from the fact that I had written a hilarious scene of the ambassador and his wife folding an American flag onstage. (No one laughed, and we threw out the scene in Philadelphia.)

The final title, *Sheep on the Runway,* was thought up by my sixteen-year-old son. He had read a line in the play about too many sheep on the runway. "Why don't you call it that?" he suggested.

"It doesn't mean anything," I said.

"So?"

"You're right," I agreed. "We'll call it *Sheep on the Runway.*"

The irony of all this was that people did think it meant something. And for months people kept coming up to me and asking, "Are we the sheep?"

And I kept saying, "Yeah."

September and October—Am meeting constantly with Gene and Bob Whitehead on script. I produce pages which they go over slowly—very slowly. Bob is perfectionist—refuses to let anything get by that he has the least doubt about. Gene is trying to find tone for play. Is it farce, burlesque, comedy, or God forbid a satire? Once we get level of it, he says, we can find the right pace.

Have rewritten script about ten times. It seems to be getting better. The question is: When will it be ready? I am nervous because it's topical and any event could knock us out of the box.

Bob and Gene are worried that it won't be right before we go into production. Roger is urging everyone to get on with it. He's ready to open next week.

It takes one hour to write a scene, two days to thrash it out with Bob and Gene. Whenever I submit pages, I wait hopefully for a reaction. If Gene doesn't like it, he raises his eyebrows or starts pulling on his beard like a Talmudic scholar. If Bob doesn't like it, he starts playing with his mustache. If both men are touching the hair on their faces, I know I'm dead.

The conferences get longer; the writing goes on. The irony of it all is I have always hated to rewrite.

While writing is going on, set designer Peter Larkin is hired to do interior of Nonomuran embassy.

THE SEARCH IS ON

The casting search is on. According to the lore of the theater, this is the best time of all for a playwright because every beautiful girl on Broadway who wants to be a star is willing to give her all to the author. It turns out this is true only of musicals.

As the casting goes on, I wonder why anyone wants the

job. A person in a straight play has to be extremely talented, out of a job, and willing to work for scale until the play opens on Broadway. He has to give up three or four months of his life to a project which he has no control over, take orders from people he hardly knows, search for something in the part that isn't there, give up a family life, and usually settle for a review which says "also in the cast was. . . ."

Casting is a cruel business.
"How about Brad Zwiback? Is he still on the bottle?"
"Forget him. I had him in *Flug*. I almost hit him."
"What about Rory Flam?"
"He can't remember his lines anymore."
"Is Rip Studebaker still alive?"
"I think he's dead. We'll have someone check into it."
"Hilda Thrush is not working at the moment."
"She's a terrible actress."
"That's what I thought. Let's not get her."
"How about Samantha Godiva?"
"She wants too much money."
"What about Glenda Rinker?"
"Christ, she's seventy-five years old."
"And Abe Misagosh?"
"Great if you want a Jewish ambassador."

I defer the casting to Bob and Gene, so I can write my column and also do the extensive rewriting. They spend hours and days hearing people they know can never make it. If they find one actor or actress in a week, they feel the time has not been wasted.

The Americans are the easiest roles to fill. Marty Gabel is perfect for the columnist, John McGiver after much persuading agrees to play the ambassador, Liz Wilson is cast as the ambassador's wife, Will MacKenzie the ambassador's aide, Margaret Ladd the ambassador's daughter. We have extraordinary luck in getting Barnard Hughes to play the general and Remak Ramsay as the AID man. Jeremiah Morris wins the role of Sam the butler.

The Nonomurans are something else again. They are almost impossible to cast, first, because we don't know what we want, and second, it's hard to find anyone Indian, Pakistani, or Chinese in the United States who can play comedy.

We finally hear about Richard Castellano, a former dock worker who has become an excellent actor in the theater. Richie is signed for the prince.

Our last problem is to cast someone to play the part of the Fort Bragg-trained Nonomuran colonel. Gene settles on a wonderful Puerto Rican actor. Unfortunately during rehearsals it turns out instead of sounding Nonomuran, our colonel sounds like Desi Arnaz. We had to replace him with an Irishman named Neil Flanagan. Someone mentions that the last time this happened the Puerto Ricans picketed the theater for weeks. As I said, casting is a cruel business.

The script is still not in shape, and Bob is hesitant to set dates. Roger and I are anxious to get it on the stage so we can have an opening night party. Gene is still trying to figure out what I've written.

My wife keeps saying to me every time I'm on my way to New York, "Aren't you glad I made them give you expenses?"

Have rewritten too many times to count. We decide to start rehearsals on November 24 at the Amsterdam Theater on Forty-second Street, in the heart of the pornography district.

2. Rehearsal

GOOD-BYE FOR A WHILE

I have kissed my family good-bye for three months. My wife is brave about it and tells her friends, "It's something Art always wanted to do, so I can't stop him."

My wife's girlfriends are very helpful.

One tells her, "I wouldn't let my husband go away for three months if he wrote *My Fair Lady*."

Another says, "Once he gets the theater bug he'll never want to come back to this boring life in Washington."

A third adds, "The theater does something to people. They have different moral standards than we do."

If a man's wife has friends, he doesn't need enemies.

I have taken a suite at the Algonquin Hotel. This is not an affectation. The Algonquin is the best hotel in the theater district, and I can walk to rehearsal. This saves taxi fares. I am getting $35 per diem while the play is in rehearsal and on the road. If I skip breakfast and lunch, I can make money on the deal.

The key to any successful play is the script girl. She has to type up the pages after they're rewritten. By the time Bob and Gene get finished with my rewrites the pages are impossible to read. The unsung heroine of this venture was a pretty young fledgling actress named Eda Zahl, who typed the script and worked the Xerox machine at outrageous hours during all our troubles and never lost her cool. Come to think of it, I should have dedicated this book to her.

THE FIRST DAY OF REHEARSAL

It's hard to believe the day has arrived—the first day that a live cast will read my lines for the first time. I feel exhilarated, optimistic, pessimistic, suspicious, and, above all, scared witless.

The cast, the director, the producers, the stage manager, the set designer, and the costume designer are seated around four tables pushed together on the cold bleak grimy stage of the New Amsterdam Roof Theater, which has been used as a rehearsal hall for many years.

These people for the next two months will be my family, my friends, my most hated enemies. Our own families, our personal responsibilities, the world outside will be shoved aside, and the only thing that will count is what each person around these tables can contribute to the play.

At the moment they are practically all strangers; in a few weeks I'll know more about each one of them than I do about my own children. We'll all be in for many surprises.

But right now everyone is holding a script, and for

the first time I really believe I'm in the theater. The reading begins. The cast breaks up at the lines, and I'm terribly grateful for such small favors. But it seems I have a lot to learn. After rehearsal Bob warned me not to take their reaction to heart. "They always laugh when reading a comedy to endear themselves to the author."

The reading goes very smoothly, and after it's over and we pose for publicity pictures that we'll never see, Gene, Bob, and I retire to the Algonquin to discuss what we've heard. The unanimous conclusion is the end of the first act doesn't work and the end of the second act doesn't work.

I slide a piece of paper into the typewriter and begin the first of a long series of rewrites that will not end until the day before opening night on Broadway.

HI THERE, PADDY

The best part of rehearsing in New York is breaking for lunch and supper at Sardi's. I've known Vince Sardi for twenty years, but this is the first time I've had anything to do with the theater, and therefore, I've earned a seat in the first section of the restaurant downstairs, which is comparable to being allowed into the queen's enclosure at Ascot.

"Hey, look. There's Paddy Chayefsky and Herb Gardner. . . . Hi, Paddy, hi, Herb. Yeah, I'm in rehearsal. Going great, just great.

"Pearl Bailey. I'm honored to meet you. . . . Do I have a part for you in my play? . . . Gosh, no, I wish I did.

"Adolph Green and Betty Comden, where? . . . Hi,

Adolph, hi, Betty. . . . Second act trouble. Nothing serious—no, wait a minute—it is serious . . . heh, heh, heh.

"Look, there's Peter Stone who wrote *1776*. Hey, Pete,
we need an actor to play a colonel.

"Say, isn't that Alan Lerner over there with Katharine
Hepburn? Hi, Alan, hi, Katey—I mean Miss Hepburn. . . .
Yup, we're right in there pitching.

"Vince, if Roger Stevens calls, tell him I've gone back
to the rehearsal hall.

"Mr. Funke, you may tell your readers that I consider
the role of the writer in the theater today. . . .

"Hey, Earl Wilson. . . . Earl, I have a very funny story
to tell you about rehearsal yesterday.

"Listen, if Hal Prince calls, tell him I couldn't wait
any longer. We're reworking the set.

"Give this note to Leonard Lyons, who's sitting over
there with Betty Bacall.

"There's no business like rehearsal business."

Observation: The happiest and most prestigious moments in a Broadway playwright's life are when he's in
rehearsal and before he opens. It is the time that almost
everyone is rooting for you, and no one knows what the
hell you've got.

Some Painful Moments

The cast is starting to ask questions about script. A
method actor wants to know: "What do I mean when I
say, 'Please come in'?"

"You mean exactly that."

"Yes, but should I say, 'Please come in,' as if I'm expecting the person or, 'Please come in,' as if I'm afraid

who it is, or, 'Please come in,' as if I didn't care who came in?"

"Ask the director," I say.

"He doesn't know."

"Well, if he doesn't and you don't, how the hell should I know?"

Ingenue is having trouble relating to the revolution she is supposed to be provoking in Nonomura. "I don't think I would say, 'Up the Prince.' "

"What would you say?" I ask her.

"I would say 'Down with the Prince.' "

"All right, say down instead of up if it makes you more comfortable."

John McGiver is worried about saying, "God damn the Voice of America," which is the opening line of the play.

I check with Bob and Gene. "Do you want to change it?" I ask them.

"No," says Bob, who has been dealing with actors all his life. "He's getting paid to say, 'God damn the Voice of America,' and he better goddamn well say it."

Marty thinks the correspondent should be more of a snob.

Everyone wants to fool with the script.

The worst part of it is that you can't ignore the cast's suggestions. Occasionally someone will come up with a line or a thought that is funnier than anything you can think of.

One of the biggest laughs in the show is a line that Richard Castellano thought of when he was horsing around in rehearsal. It came when the ambassador said,

"The President's on the phone," and Richie said, "Oh, let me speak to Pat."

Marty Gabel and John McGiver, both very intelligent men, point out several blatant flaws in the script. Remak Ramsay, a Princeton graduate, also makes some very valuable contributions, and Barnard Hughes, who plays the general and is one of the best professional actors in the theater, comes up with some excellent business.

The trick I discover is to keep the cast from rewriting the script, at the same time listening to everything that is said.

Another thing you learn is not to get too friendly with the actors or they'll eat you for supper.

"There's a telephone call from your sister."

"Hello."

"Arthur, I don't want to bother you when you're writing your play."

"Uh-huh."

"But Mrs. Kaplan, whom I'm sitting with, was wondering if she could have eight seats to the opening night. She says she'll pay for them."

"Who the hell is Mrs. Kaplan?"

"You met her at my house four years ago. Remember, her husband is in the roofing business and they were telling us about their trip to Puerto Rico? She wants to make it perfectly clear that she'll pay for the seats."

"I don't have any extra seats for opening night. I don't

have enough seats for my friends. Tell her I'll see that she gets seats on another night, any other night."

"Just a minute. . . . She says the only night she's interested in is opening night. She wants it understood that she doesn't want them free."

"It isn't a question of paying for them or not. I don't have the seats. Ask her if she wants to go the night after?"

"Hold on. . . . No, she says to forget it. . . . Wait a minute. She wants to know if you understand that she isn't asking for passes. She can send you a check in the morning."

"Please, I do not have any seats."

"All right. . . ."

"Now what did she say?"

"She said . . . she said it's strange how people forget their friends when they become important."

We have been in rehearsal for two weeks. I am holed up at the Algonquin writing new scenes and lines. Every night I have new pages for Gene and Bob to go over. Now that we've done so much work on the play and have been in rehearsal for fourteen days, someone brings up the question that I always knew would come up sooner or later.

"What is the play all about?"

I stammer and stutter, " I don't know."

"Is it about Holly and Fred or about war or about mankind going down on the *Titanic?*" Bob asks.

"Yes," I say. "That's it."

"The trouble, as I see it," says Gene, "is that we have to make our people more interesting because otherwise *we* lose interest."

"Exactly," I say.

"The character Holly, as you have her written now, is a pain in the ass," Bob says.

"I hate her myself," I agree.

"Fred is a bore," Gene says.

"A bloody bore," I agree.

"And the end still doesn't work."

"You can say that again," I murmur.

"Damn it," says Bob. "How can we ever get anywhere if you don't defend yourself?"

"Am I supposed to?"

"Of course," says Gene, disgusted. "At this stage the writer is supposed to be so damned mad at the producer and director he isn't even talking to them."

"But I love both of you."

"It's impossible to work with you," Gene shouts. "You give in too easy."

"We don't know what works any more than you do. Someone in this trio has to have confidence. We were counting on you for that," Bob says.

"I was counting on both of *you*."

"Jesus," Gene says. "What do we do now?"

"I wish to say," I announce, "that I think you don't know balls about the theater."

"That's more like it," Bob says.

"And I've decided that instead of working anymore tonight, I'm going out to see a dirty movie on Forty-second Street."

"Bravo!" says Gene. "I knew you'd turn into a bastard sooner or later."

Broadway is a sea of pornography. It's hard to concentrate because every time I look around there's words like "lust," "perversion," "screw," "fuck," "whips," "deflowering." They're in the window of every bookstore, on every newsstand, and over almost every movie theater. The words have been working on me subliminally, and I keep inserting them into the script.

I don't know what to do. The play has no nudity, no lesbians, no homosexuals. Could it be a breakthrough in the theater?

I thought I was prepared for everything. But one night at twelve o'clock while I'm writing in my room, I receive a telephone call from a lady who identifies herself as being with the theater wing of SANE, the antiwar organization.

"Mr. Buchward, do you know that one of your backers manufactures napalm?"

I drop the pastrami sandwich I'm holding in my hand. "Oh."

"Yes. Mr. Robert Dowling is chairman of the Board of the City Investing Company, and they just bought a chemical company in California that has the napalm contract."

"You've got to be kidding."

"I'm not. And we had a meeting last night and we've decided to picket City Investing. Some of the more militant groups at the meeting also want to picket your play."

"But I've written an antiwar play."

"We know that, and some of the people who attended the meeting have read the script, and they feel it would be wrong to picket your play; but I can't guarantee you that the militants will not go ahead with their plans."

"Are they going to picket the New Amsterdam Theater where we're in rehearsal?" I ask.

"I suppose so."

"My God. They can't. They'll be mugged by all the perverts on Forty-second Street!"

"Well, we've decided for the moment to picket only the City Investing Company at the General Motors Building. As a matter of fact, a group of us who are for the play have decided to carry signs saying that *Sheep on the Runway* is okay."

"Please, lady, don't do it. It will look like a bad publicity stunt. Don't carry any signs. Leave us out of it."

"Well, I thought you would just like to know."

"Thank you and good luck at the General Motors Building."

I call Bob. "Do you know Dowling makes napalm?"

"Oh, no. Who told you?"

"A lady from SANE."

"Are you drunk?"

"No, but if you have any class, you'll be out on the picket line tomorrow morning in front of the General Motors Building."

"Go to sleep."

"And bring a picket sign." I hang up. I pick up my pastrami sandwich off the floor. The bread still seems to be clean.

Postscript: SANE did picket the next day at the GM Building, but they left us out of it.

Our Prince, Richard Castellano, is not giving a performance during the rehearsal. He has been trained in the method school of acting and says he can't do his part without feeling it. How can a former longshoreman know how a Himalayan prince feels? I suggest to Bob and Gene we send him to Nepal for six months to get the hang of it. But we're very discouraged, and we feel he's bringing everyone else down.

For two weeks now we've been suffering with him, and finally we decide he has to be fired. This is a very expensive proposition because he has a run-of-the-play contract and gets $1,000 a week. This means for every week *Sheep* plays he gets $1,000, while we have to pay another actor to play the part.

But there doesn't seem to be anything else to do. He won't get with it.

Gene blows up at him, and he blows up at Gene, and they have a shouting match. After that he gives a better performance. But he still doesn't know his lines.

The decision is made. We have to find a new Prince. During lunch hour we sneak over to the Billy Rose Theater to audition actors. Any one of them sounds better than Castellano. We finally settle on a very fine English

actor named Roderick Cook. Castellano will play the part
in New Haven, and then we'll put Roderick in. It's decided. Richie is informed. We all feel bad about it. But
you have to be tough in show business, particularly when
you know you're right.

Postscript: We opened with Castellano in New Haven
and he gave a brilliant performance and walked away with
all the best reviews. So we had to fire Roderick and rehire
Castellano.

I made a mental note never to fire a method actor again
until *after* opening night.

Broadway and Forty-sixth Street. Noon.
"Say, aren't you Art Buchwald?"
"Yeah."
"My name is Phil Conable. I knew you when you were
a kid. I used to date your sister."
"Yeah."
"Remember at that time I asked you what you wanted
to be. . . . You couldn't have been more than nine or ten.
Remember what you told me?"
"I forget."
"You said you wanted to be a writer."
"Oh, yeah."
"Remember what I told you?"
"I'm not sure."
"I said if you want to be a writer, be one."
"Yeah."

Counting Sheep

"Well, I hope you don't mind, but I've told everyone I started you in your career."

"Thanks a lot."

"I don't want credit. I was glad I could be of help."

38

3. New Haven

"This is the state police. We are advising all drivers to stay off the roads and highways because of dangerous icy weather conditions. We repeat, stay off the roads unless you have urgent business."

This announcement, or one similar to it, was repeated every night we played in New Haven at the Shubert Theater. You can imagine how great this evening commercial was for business.

Some excerpts from my diary:

Sunday, December 21, 1969

Our first live audience has shown up for a dress rehearsal. Four hundred people in the Shubert Theater, which seats 2,500. It's a disaster! We're in so much trouble we can't believe it. The audience is frightened. The audience refuses to buy the basic situation. The flag folding doesn't work; the references to Vietnam seem grim. We're saying something no one wants to laugh at. But it all sounded so funny in rehearsal!

Bob, Gene, and Roger are as confused as I am. Nothing about the play seems right. NOTHING. It's such a mess there's got to be hope somewhere. I think I'd better check the airline schedules out of here.

Counting Sheep

Monday, December 22, 1969. Opening night

The driving force in the theater is fear. Haven't felt like this since I got off a U.S. marine landing boat at Eniwetok during World War II.

Things were better than last night. For one thing we almost had a full house. They laughed during the first act and we got off to a good start. As I said, Richie Castellano, whom we were going to fire, is brilliant. The trouble seems to be with the Joe Mayflower role. He is too sinister. The audience hates him and refuses to laugh. I've got to make the audience like Mayflower.

The last half of the second act fell apart. Once the tanks arrived for the *coup d'état* everyone in the theater froze.

The audience seems good-natured until the war starts. The goddamn sound effects we've set up around the theater, in stereo no less, are making people hold onto their seats. They couldn't be more amused unless we were hijacking them to Cuba.

We just had one of those all-night sessions in my room that look funny when you see them in the movies, but are pretty grim in real life.

There is a plane leaving at nine o'clock tomorrow morning from New Haven with connections to Brazil. I found out from a friend that they can't extradite you from Brazil if you've written a flop.

Tuesday, December 23, 1969

Jingle bells, jingle bells, jingle all the way. The reviews are in. They're not as bad as we thought they'd be.

Morning New Haven *Register* has reservations, but

liked it. Afternoon paper, which is most important for theater, did not. Hartford paper likes it. *Variety* says we have something but doesn't know what.

I've been calling everyone all day in New York and Washington telling them we got raves. Might as well have the rumor factories spread good news rather than bad.

(NOTE: I learned since then that good news about plays does not travel, while bad news spreads instantaneously to every portion of the globe. My attempt at bravado failed. Much later I discovered everyone knew we were in trouble in New Haven, and those who didn't know it assumed as much.)

Christmas Eve, December 24, 1969

No one in the theater on Christmas Eve. We're playing to people who can't stand Christmas at home. They're as depressed as we are. No one should have to spend Christmas Eve in New Haven, not even people who live there. As I walked out of the theater tonight into the snow, an old lady near the door said, "Don't worry, Mr. Buchwald, it will get better."

All I could say was: "And a Merry Christmas to you."

If Santa Claus would only come down the chimney and give me fifty good jokes, I'd never ask another thing from him again.

GOD BLESS YOU, MERRY GENTLEMEN

Christmas Day

New Haven is under a blanket of snow. The hotel has promised us breakfast but has warned us that as far as food is concerned, we're on our own for the rest of the day. At ten thirty I call down for room service. The girl says the room service waiters haven't come in—there is no breakfast.

I dress and go downstairs to the lobby.

"What's open?" I ask the sole employee in the hotel.

"The White Tower," she says, pointing her finger out at the snow. "You usually can see it from the corner, but I guess you can't today."

I trudge over to the White Tower, which is jammed with people, and after twenty minutes I grab a stool. The two waitresses hash over their holiday blues and seem to be ignoring all but their closest friends. I am getting madder and madder. Finally I say, "Can I get some service around here?"

A man pops out from behind the range and snarls, "If you don't like it here, Mac, get the hell out."

Oh, Christ, I think to myself. *I'm being kicked out of a White Tower on Christmas Day.*

My stomach tells me to stay but my pride says, "Go." I get up off the stool as I imagine John Wayne would do it, hitch up my pants, and walk toward the door. Everyone is watching. I turn and look at them with my steely eyes and say, "Howard Johnson will hear about this." Then out into the snow and cold before I faint in the joint.

As I trudge back to the hotel, chewing on my lip for sustenance, I remember that Kingman Brewster, the president of Yale, and his wife had invited me for Christmas dinner about a week ago. I had no intention of crashing in on their family affair until just then.

I rush back to the hotel and call him.

"Is that invitation still open for Christmas dinner?"

"Yes, it is," he replies.

"Please," I beg, " don't start without me."

No supplicant at a Salvation Army Christmas dinner is as grateful as I am for the Brewster turkey and trimmings. I am willing to pray, sing, or write praises for Yale. I keep thanking everyone for passing the plates my way.

Stuffed and content, I return to the theater for rehearsal only to discover that the cast has not eaten all day.

"Where have you been?" Gene asks.

I can't lie. "I had Christmas dinner at the Kingman Brewsters'."

Gene looks at me and says, "You son of a bitch."

December 27, 1969, our last night in New Haven

Gene is furious at cast. None of them is playing the part. I tell Gene to give them the Knute Rockne speech. If all else fails, I tell him to tell the cast that my nephew is coming tonight.

For the first time the play played, and I feel we have a chance. The audience liked it very much, the laughs were there, and we had a full house. I got the feeling of elation and excitement which, after the depression we've all been in, has renewed my faith in the project. Good-bye, New Haven.

PHILADELPHIA, HERE WE COME.

4. Philadelphia

THEY LOVE ME IN PHILADELPHIA

December 29, 1969

Every joke, story, or nasty crack you've ever heard about Philadelphia is true—that is, if you open a play in this town and you get very bad reviews.

We opened tonight at the New Locust Theater, a barn-like building much too large for a straight comedy. (I wonder if I would have written that if the critics had liked the show.)

The natives seemed friendly as they came into the theater. But the nearer it got to curtain time, the more nervous I became. I wished we had never left New Haven. At least there it was snowing and I could blame all my troubles on the weather.

I learned in New Haven not to hang around the lobby of the theater during intermission, because too many people wanted to tell me what was wrong with the play.

So in Philadelphia I ducked backstage during intermission and had to depend on Seymour Krawitz, the press agent, for the comments. Seymour came back and reported all the comments in the lobby were good. (I discovered only after we opened in New York that Seymour never hears bad comments on a play he is representing as the press agent.)

But when the curtain went down at the end of the show, no one in the company seemed truly happy. We went back to the Barclay Hotel to sweat out the Philadelphia *Inquirer*'s review.

By the time I got to Bob Whitehead's suite the review had been phoned in, and Bob, Gene, Bob's wife, Zoe Caldwell, and Seymour were glumly sitting around. Their faces told me all I had to know.

William Collins, the *Inquirer*'s critic, started the piece: "Art Buchwald could find material for six months in a comedy called 'Sheep on the Runway.' His problem at the moment is making it into a play. . . ." From there on it was all downhill.

The Philadelphia *News* review came in a few minutes later. Charles Petzold wrote: "It is painfully obvious that Buchwald has taken his column type humor and tried to stretch it into a full length play. . . ." No quotes for the ads from Mr. Petzold.

"There's still the *Bulletin*," Seymour said hopefully.

"Of course, the *Bulletin*. They print my column," I said. "Surely the *Bulletin* will like it."

We can't get a review of the *Bulletin* until the following morning. At least we can dream that the *Bulletin* will save us.

December 30, 1969

Was I wrong about the *Bulletin!* If the critics of the *Inquirer* and *News* disliked the play, Ernest Schier loathed it. Not only did he loathe the play, but it turned out from the review he also loathed me.

How about this for openers? "The feeling I got watching 'Sheep on the Runway' is that for years people have been telling Art Buchwald that he's such a funny writer why doesn't he write a play.

"So he did. . . . My question, Art, is didn't anybody ever ask you not to write a play, some jealous brother-in-law, or your accountant? To them you should have listened."

And in case I didn't get the point, Mr. Schier ended his love letter to me by saying, "Just to be safe maybe you'd better pay a courtesy call on the 450 editors who run your column. A fellow never knows when he'll need a friend."

The toughest thing to do when you've been clobbered by the critics out of town is face the cast. There is really nothing you can say except "What the hell do they know in Philadelphia?"

But the trouble with that line is if someone says it to you first, you don't have an answer.

I went to the New Locust with my head bloodied and bowed. I had the flu with all my other difficulties, but I knew if I didn't show, they would think I was deserting the ship. So I walked into the theater, said my "What the hell do they know in Philadelphia?" as some choirboy would say his "Hail Marys" and then went back to my room to vomit in peace.

December 31, 1969

My flu has turned into a liver ailment. It could be hepatitis. My eyes are yellow.

Could the reviews have given me yellow jaundice?

I can't keep any food down.

Bob and Gene are very worried. We have a tremendous amount of work to do in Philadelphia, and if I've got hepatitis, they haven't got a playwright.

My priorities seemed to have changed. I don't care if the play folds. I just don't want my liver to close out of town.

January 2, 1970

I don't know what happened to New Year's Day. I think it took place. The doctor insists that anyone who has been in contact with me has to take gamma globulin shots. This means Bob, Gene, Zoe, and their little baby, Sam.

Bob, who has been in the theater a long long time, says he's been in trouble on the road before, but he has never seen anything like this.

While I don't like being sick, I try to look on the bright side of things. If we're going to close in Philly at least we have a good cover story: "PLAYWRIGHT'S LIVER AILMENT FORCES POSTPONEMENT OF 'SHEEP ON THE RUNWAY' (Forever)."

The tests are inconclusive. I have hepatitis—I don't have hepatitis. I know the second act needs work, but how do you do it if you can't keep your soup down?

I'm not one to hold a grudge, but why couldn't the

critic of the *Bulletin* have gotten liver trouble instead of me?

EVERYONE'S A CRITIC

DEAR MR. BUCHWALD,
  Last night my wife, two friends, and myself had a series of arguments on various subjects.
  Then we saw your show.
  Mr. Buchwald . . . you brought us together.
  We were all unhappy with the performance. And happy that we could agree on something.

Sincerely,
ELLIOTT R. CURSON
Elliott Curson Advertising
Philadelphia, Pennsylvania

DEAR ART:
  As an old reader and appreciator of your humor, I paid American money for five tickets to take my family to see your show *Sheep on the Runway* (orchestra seats), and in spite of the rave reviews, we turned up loyally on a bitter cold Thursday night, January 8 to be exact.
  I was willing to accept the risk that you might not be as good a playwright as you are a columnist, but I did not bargain for a one-act performance with an assistant stage manager reading the leading part from a book. The only fair comment on the play is that you must be rewriting it before taking it to New York.
  I thought of leading a demonstration against this unfair treatment of your loyal supporters; but the play was

over too soon, and I did not have an intermission to re-
flect on it.

The least you can do is send me tickets to see whatever
it is that comes out in New York, but if you insist on re-
funding the price of the tickets, I will accept it.

Sincerely yours,
HARVEY B. LEVIN
Attorney at Law
Philadelphia, Pennsylvania

January 5, 1970

I've been confined to my room at the Barclay. Bob and
Gene are very worried (discovered later they were seriously considering closing the show. We weren't doing any
business, and no one could tell them when I'd be on my
feet).

We met in the room, and I finally said the words they
were hoping I would: "If you guys want to call in someone to help us, it's all right with me." In the jargon of the
trade the "someone" is known as a play doctor. More
shows than anyone would like to admit have been doc-
tored out of town. It's tough on the ego of the playwright
to have someone come in at this stage, but many plays
have failed because the writer was too proud to ask for
help.

Gene says he thinks he can get Joe Stein, who wrote
the book for *Fiddler on the Roof* and *Zorba*, to come
down and tell us what is wrong. I know Joe Stein slightly,
respect his work, and I'm agreeable to anyone coming in,
just as long as I can keep a meal down.

January 6, 1970

The play doctor has arrived. He doesn't have a black bag. He doesn't even have a clean shirt. He says he's just come to look at the play and see what is wrong. Then he's going back to New York.

After the play everyone gathers back at my room.

We all defer to Joe.

He says, "The play needs a major rewrite."

I could have told him that, sick as I am.

"The part of the correspondent is too straight. We have to make him completely paranoid—an absolute madman. The ending has to go. [I believe we tried twelve different endings after that.] And you need a lot more jokes."

Joe agrees to work with me on fixing up the play. It means I have to give him 2 percent of my 10 percent share of the royalties. But he says he wants no credit. The terms are agreeable. His agent, William Morris, is my agent, so the haggling is kept to a minimum. Whatever fighting goes on is between his/my agent and Bob Whitehead.

January 7, 1970

The collaborating is going well. Joe is very easy to work with, and it's fun to have someone to talk to. He knows how to shape a scene and build toward a laugh, something I apparently have yet to learn. He has some great ideas, he has some terrible ideas, but I notice that anything he suggests Gene and Bob will buy, while anything I suggest now meets with resistance. From now on I feed all my ideas through Joe so they'll be accepted.

Rule of the theater: The guy who came in last is the one everyone listens to.

A FEW WORDS ABOUT FRIENDS WHO VISIT YOU OUT OF TOWN

One of the reasons people go out of town to try out plays is that they won't be bothered by relatives, friends, and people in the theater.

Many well-meaning pals decide, on their own, to take the long, arduous trip to New Haven, Boston, or Philadelphia to give aid and comfort to those who are suffering.

Each, in his own way, manages to shake up the production more than it is already. There's nothing that someone on the road suffering from physical and mental exhaustion likes to hear less than the opinions of an outsider on why the show is in trouble.

FRIEND OF PLAYWRIGHT: You know the director has screwed up your play.

PLAYWRIGHT: No kidding.

F.O.P.: It's dull, unimaginative, pedestrian direction.

PLAYWRIGHT: You think so?

F.O.P.: What have I got to gain by lying to you?

FRIEND OF DIRECTOR: You did a brilliant job with what you had to work with.

DIRECTOR: You don't like the play?

F.O.D.: I like what *you* did. But you have to have a script. You're not a miracle man.

DIRECTOR: Thanks for coming.

F.O.D.: Why wouldn't I come?

ACTOR'S AGENT: Is this what they gave you for a dressing room?

ACTOR: Why, isn't it all right?

AGENT: It's a slum. If I knew they were going to treat you like this, I would have never let you take the part.

ACTOR: I really don't mind it.

AGENT: I hear they cut your lines last night.

ACTOR: Just two.

AGENT: They're not going to get away with it. They're going to show you some respect. I didn't come all the way down to Philadelphia to have them shove you around.

FRIEND OF PRODUCER: It has a lot of good things in it, Roger, but if you ask my opinion, you're in trouble.

PRODUCER: How can I get out of trouble?

F.O.P.: Start over with a new writer, a new director, and a new cast. Keep the elements that are good and throw out everything else.

PRODUCER: That could get expensive.

F.O.P.: I know, but you're talking like a man who has a choice.

PRODUCER: You staying overnight?

F.O.P.: No, I have to go to Detroit. I understand David is in trouble with Monsoon and I want to be as helpful as I can.

Despite the difficulties the Penn Central had last winter, many people who wouldn't have gone to Larchmont made it to Philadelphia to tell what was wrong with our show.

January 8, 1970

Just when the writing seemed to going well, disaster has struck the production. John McGiver has been taken to the hospital, and nobody knows what's wrong with him. The assistant stage manager, Howard Fisher, is walking around the stage during matinee and evening perform-ance with a script in his hand reading McGiver's part. How long? Oh, Lord, how long?

We have to postpone the opening in New York, not only because we're inserting new material every day that actors have to learn, but because we may not have a star.

Friday, January 9, 1970

I got good marks on my liver. Apparently whatever second-act trouble I was having with it has disappeared. The doc says I can go to New York and stay with the play. There goes my last excuse to get out of this mess with honor.

Saturday, January 10, 1970

The verdict is in on McGiver. He has pleurisy. Seems it's an old ailment that comes back every once in a while. It's serious enough for his medicine man to rule out John's continuing in the show.

This is our last night in Philly. Gene, Joe Stein, and I can't stand what we're looking at on the stage, so we leave in the middle of the first act and take a limousine that Roger has provided for us back to New York. There are no laughs in the car.

We're not insured against McGiver's illness. We start discussing replacements. Most of the people we want are dead, making movies, or in alcoholic sanitariums. We don't have a prayer of getting someone in the next week.

One gets the feeling that the gods are angry. But why me?

Oh, I almost forgot to say good-bye to Philadelphia. Good-bye, Philly. I wouldn't live in your town even if you had a good baseball team.

5. New York

I'm back at the Algonquin. It's like coming home. Everyone is friendly, glad to see me. The Algonquin is a unique institution. It lives and breathes show business. The valet can talk plot with you; the bellmen have a sincere rooting interest in the show. Ben Bodne and his wife and his son-in-law and his grandchildren all are theater buffs. The headwaiters, room service waiters, and telephone operators are rooting me on. Mr. Hilton and Mr. Sheraton can build their giant glass computerized palaces, but they can't give you the love you get at the Algonquin.

No luck with McGiver's replacement. Jack Albertson is on the coast—not available. Hiram Sherman is in England. What about Tony Randall? Tony Randall is doing something else.

Paul Ford wants to do it! How about that? His agent says he's free. Paul Ford is great. Paul is marvelous. Let's hear it for Paul Ford.

Monday, January 12, 1970

Paul Ford showed up for rehearsal. He's not as young as we thought he was. He's been ill. The part would kill

55

him. The ambassador is on during the entire show. Why didn't someone at least meet Ford before we signed him? Bob calls Ford's agent: "Look, we all made a mistake. . . ."

Christ, we still don't have a lead, and tomorrow we start previews.

Most shows have preview performances before opening night. They can range from five to fifty, depending on how much trouble you're in.

Preview tickets are sold at a dollar or two less to attract an audience. But the truth of the matter is that unless you have a sensational hit with great out-of-town reviews, you rarely sell enough tickets and must therefore paper the house—that is, give out free seats every night.

You would think it would be easy to give away free seats to the theater. But the sad fact is that even free tickets are not enough of an inducement to bring in a crowd.

One night during previews, when things were as bad as they could possibly be, I walked to the Helen Hayes and saw several buses in front of the theater.

David Hedges, the company manager, said, "Do you know who's in the theater tonight?"

"I have no idea."

"Two hundred patients from a mental hospital."

"Oh."

"Well, not exactly two hundred. There are one hundred and ninety-nine. One is missing. We're looking for him now."

I walked into the theater.

David said, "You don't have anything to worry about. They're all tranquilized."

"I'm not worried, David," I said. "But suppose they go back to the hospital and tell their friends they liked it?"

I just saw Arlene Francis, Marty Gabel's wife. She gave me a big hug and a kiss. "You'll never know how grateful I am to you," she said. "You got Marty out of the house."

January 15, 1970

We have an ambassador. David Burns, one of the best, funniest, and finest actors in the theater, has been talked into playing the part by Bob Whitehead.

Davey had been ill and didn't want to work. But he saw the play, liked it, and now he's going to do it. Gene and Joe Stein are ecstatic. It's going to change the play from a satire to a farce, which they claim it should have been all the time. It will take Davey ten days to learn and rehearse the part. (The big question people always ask when replacing an actor is: "Is he a quick study?" Which means: Can he learn his lines fast?)

Joe and I are still working on the ending and the Joe Mayflower part. We start at ten, work till noon, talk about girls until three, read the stuff to Gene and Bob at five, and then go back and work it over some more.

One night we broke about seven, and I said I couldn't work because I was going to visit my folks. "That's good," said Joe. "Because I want to spend the evening with my son."

We said good-bye.

I noticed in the paper that *Without a Stitch,* an erotic Danish picture, was playing at the Loew's State and decided to go. When the lights went on after the picture was over I bumped into Joe coming up the aisle.

"How are your folks?" he said.

"Fine," I said. "How's your son?"

"Good," he said.

"If you don't tell Bob on me, I won't tell Gene on you."

We went to the Gaiety Delicatessen to seal the deal.

L'AFFAIRE ALSOP

One of the by-products of *Sheep* was the making of an enemy for life. Joseph Alsop is a distinguished political columnist, of impeccable taste, family connections (he's related to the Roosevelts), and with very strong opinions on how we should conduct our foreign affairs. He has always been a strong supporter of our military posture throughout the world and has had little patience with those who happen to be less hawkish than he is about the wars we get involved in.

Alsop has been one of our most optimistic reporters on Vietnam and probably has seen the light at the end of the tunnel more than any other syndicated columnist in the business.

Joe commutes between the United States and Vietnam the way other people commute between Great Neck and New York. His in-depth analyses of the situation in Indochina have made him the darling of the Pentagon, the confidant of Presidents, and the unofficial scolder of those who believe Vietnam was a big mistake.

As Washington's official "Voice of Doom," he livens up our dull town, and we're all grateful for the joy he brings to our breakfast table three times a week.

When I decided to write the play, I chose as one of the major characters a fictitious hawk columnist whom I named Joseph Mayflower—the Joseph after my good friend Joseph Kraft and the Mayflower after the ship our ancestors came on.

Joe Mayflower became the catalytic agent who starts the play on its bumpy way to insanity. For some reason, which I'll never fathom, Joseph Alsop thought I had patterned my main character after him.

From friends I gathered that first he thought it was a joke and even intended to come to the opening. But while I was out of town with my finger in the dike, my "friends" and his were hard at work, giving Joe the needle about the play.

One dear friend, Rowland Evans, spent an entire evening with Alsop in Washington asking him what he intended to do about my play. Alsop, who up to that point said he intended to do nothing about it, finally told Rowland in a rage that anyone who went to the opening of *Sheep* could no longer be considered a friend of his. He said his friends and mine would have to choose between us.

This declaration was made in front of enough people that it reached the ears of Maxine Cheshire, the Washington *Post* gossip columnist, whom Alsop later described as the *Post*'s own "House Bitch."

She printed it as the lead item in her column, and suddenly war was declared.

I started getting calls at the Algonquin from all the press media asking me what I had to say. (There hadn't been a good feud in the newspaper business since Westbrook Pegler zonked Quentin Reynolds and vice versa.)

I insisted that my character was a notorious hawk snob and bore no resemblance to my dear friend Joe Alsop. I said I was hurt and appalled that Mr. Alsop would think I would put a character on the stage that in any way would look or sound like him.

I wrote a letter to the Washington *Post* expressing shock at Miss Cheshire's item.

When *Time* magazine asked me if I would invite Alsop to the opening, I said that I'd love to but I never invited columnists to any opening nights of my plays.

I went out of my way on television and in interviews denying I had any of Joe Alsop in *Sheep on the Runway.* The press agent wanted to make publicity hay with the feud, but I said, "No, I refuse to take advantage of this unfortunate misunderstanding." I authorized him to release that statement to both Associated and United Press.

But despite my denials, Alsop decided to hire an attorney, and through Bob Kintner, former president of NBC, he obtained the services of William Fitelson, the distinguished show business lawyer.

On a Saturday matinee before the preview Mr. Fitelson showed up at the Helen Hayes Theater to see the play.

I wasn't there, but Fitelson told Bob Whitehead before the curtain went up that he was representing Mr. Alsop and would settle for the following demands: that I change the name of the character from Joseph Mayflower to somebody else and that I write letters to *Time, Newsweek, New York* magazine, *Life,* and the New York *Times* stating that there was no resemblance between my character and Joseph Alsop except for the fact they both were hawks. Only after I agreed to this would they decide whether they were going to sue me or not. Fitelson also said—and this really hurt—that he wasn't too concerned because he understood the play was a bomb and wouldn't last a week.

Bob passed on this conversation to me at the Algonquin, and I decided that I had to take some defensive measures. So I called my dear friend Edward Bennett Williams, the famous Washington lawyer who has defended such varied people as Adam Clayton Powell, Frank Costello, Senator Joe McCarthy, Bobby Baker, and Frank Sinatra. Eddie belongs to the same club I do, which is made up of three members: Williams, Benjamin Bradlee, the editor of the Washington *Post,* and myself. We meet once a week for lunch, and the sole purpose of the club is to keep other people out. We each propose members we'd like to let in and then vote on them. Inevitably someone blackballs whoever is proposed. This way we keep a perfect ethnic balance. Eddie is Catholic, Benjy is a WASP, and my dog tag says I'm a Hebrew.

As soon as I told Eddie what had transpired, he became elated. He had heard about the notices in Philadelphia and said, "Alsop might save your show after all."

This stung, but I didn't say anything because I didn't want to lose him as a lawyer.

"The first thing we'll do is take a deposition from him asking why he thinks the maniac you've written about in your play bears any resemblance to Alsop. We'll keep him on the stand for two days. Then we'll agree that we will announce before each performance that the news-

paperman in our play has nothing to do with Joseph
Alsop, the columnist. Furthermore, we will take out advertisements stating this."

"That's great. Does he have a suit?"

"No chance. But if he wants to sue, we must not look
a gift horse in the mouth," Eddie said.

"One more question. How much is this going to cost
me?" I asked.

"I am taking this on behalf of the Legal Aid Society of
Georgetown."

I breathed a sigh of relief. When the next newspaperman called me I said, "I must refer all questions concerning this unfortunate misunderstanding to my well-known
Washington attorney, Mr. Edward Bennett Williams."

I also called Robert Montgomery (no relation to the
actor), who was the Stevens-Whitehead lawyer, and told
him, "Tell Fitelson the next time he calls that my attorney, Mr. Edward Bennett Williams, will be happy to
discuss any grievances with him."

I don't know if Fitelson was frightened off by Williams
or if he decided he had no case, but he never called Williams to make any official demands.

In the meantime, back in Washington, unbeknownst to
me, the town was buzzing (well, the salons of Georgetown
anyway) about the Alsop-Buchwald feud.

Alsop was getting calls from newspapermen, too, and
after one from a reporter from the Washington *Post* he
called up Benjamin Bradlee, an old friend, who happened to be my old friend, and told Bradlee that he was
sick and tired of the publicity.

Bradlee decided to arbitrate the dispute. The first
thing he did was call my wife, who up until then had

been pretty good about my being away from home. He told my dear wife that he was very concerned with my reputation in Washington because everyone was talking about what a rat I was for calling my main character Joe Mayflower. Bradlee said that up until then my reputation had been unblemished by scandal, but now I was to go down in history as a slanderer of hawk columnists.

My wife has nothing but respect for Bradlee and believes everything he tells her, so she immediately called me at eleven o'clock that night and said she had received this call from Bradlee and she was very worried because everyone in Washington was talking about me. She said that she was ashamed to go out and run into people after what I had done, and she wasn't going to leave the house until the play opened.

She also said she was fed up with being a playwright's widow, and she said if I had any respect for her and my children, I would change the name of Joe Mayflower that night.

I explained to her that I wanted to, but my actors had a great deal of trouble learning their lines and I could never change Joe's name without lousing up my play.

She was very understanding about this and hung up on me.

I got word back to Bradlee that he had screwed up my married life and I was thinking of resigning from the club.

But Bradlee decided to make one more pitch for Joe. He made an appointment to see Williams at his office with Philip Geyelin, the Washington *Post* editor of the editorial page, a dear friend of mine and Joe Alsop's.

Eddie told me what took place.

Bradlee opened up by saying, "Eddie, I am worried

about Artie. All his friends in Washington are furious at him for maligning Joe Alsop. We've got to save him."

"How do you suggest we do this?" Eddie said, taking out a yellow lined pad and pencil.

"You've got to talk Artie into changing the name of his main character."

"Why is that?" Eddie asked.

"Because Artie's reputation is at stake."

Geyelin was trying to keep a straight face.

"Would you be good enough to tell me the names of these friends who are so disturbed by what Artie has done?"

Bradlee was stumped. Finally he said, "Ethel Kennedy, if she knew about it."

Geyelin started breaking up.

Eddie said, "Benjy, if Artie were a friend, I would certainly do everything in my power to persuade him to make the necessary changes. But Artie isn't my friend. He's my client. And as my client the only thing I can advise him to do is take the demands and tell Joe to—"

Just then the phone rang. It was Katharine Graham, the publisher of the Washington *Post,* calling from Barbados. Benjy got on the phone and said, "No, he isn't buying any of it."

Bradlee and Geyelin left the office in despair with Williams yelling after them, "You have to understand. I'm protecting my client."

I heard no more from Alsop after that. But after the show opened his brother Stewart went and reviewed it for the *Post.*

He said in part . . .

Joe Mayflower is not funny. As the New York Times reviewer noted, he is "poisonously stupid and arrogant." No one who knows him would deny that the real Mayflower occasionally displays what Winston Churchill called "a little honest arrogance." But stupid?

Buchwald's Mayflower is not only stupid. He is a hissing villain, a buffoon with blood on his hands. He wholly lacks the qualities that have made a vast collection of friends—including both John and Robert Kennedy—for the real Mayflower. He also lacks the qualities—notably the courage to be unfashionable—that have made Joe Mayflower a great reporter. It is not surprising that Joe Mayflower should emerge, in Buchwald's fashionable farce, as a caricature. It is surprising—for Art Buchwald has always seemed an amiable fellow—that the caricature should be so bitchy.

After it appeared I wrote Stewart a note saying: "If *you* say it isn't Joe and *I* say it isn't Joe—then let's get the son of a bitch who says it *is* Joe."

I have to assume the Alsop feud will go on, whether I want it to or not. After the play opened and everything presumably calmed down, I was back in Washington when six of my suits were stolen from the kitchen. I reported it to the police, and the story, for comic relief, made the front page of the Washington *Star*. The Washington *Post* felt obligated to find a new angle for its next morning's edition, so one of its reporters called up Joe Alsop and said, "Mr. Alsop, did you steal Buchwald's suits?"

Witnesses say Alsop's scream was heard across the Potomac in Virginia.

Counting Sheep

SEYMOUR KRAWITZ AND COMPANY—Publicity

TO: Art Buchwald

Following is your schedule of interviews for Monday and Tuesday:

MONDAY

10:00 AM	MARTHA DEAN SHOW	WOR, 1440 Broadway, 24th floor
11:30 AM	FRED ROBBINS SHOW	Twenty-minute taping at 206 East 58th Street
12:30 AM	BILL RAIDY	Lunch interview at Oak Room, Algonquin
2:00 PM	EMORY LEWIS	Interview at the Algonquin
3:30 PM	HELEN HALL	30 minutes to interview for radio at RFT, Inc., 43 West 54th Street. This is syndicated to 500 stations
6:15 PM	NEWSFRONT WNDT-TV (Ch. 13)	Taped at 345 East 46th Street. About 30 minutes

TUESDAY

9:45 AM	CASPER CITRON	Radio taping at Room 306, Algonquin
10:00 AM	DAPHNE KRAFT	Interview for Newark *News* —Algonquin
10:45 AM	JOHN TUCKER	Taping for John's half-hour Sunday show on ABC-TV. Taped at Studio TV 11, corner 67th Street and Central Park West (in Des Artistes Hotel)

Seymour will meet you in the lobby of WOR, 1440 Broadway, at 9:50 Monday.

We had no advance sale on *Sheep*. It turns out that it's difficult to get an advance on a straight play particularly when the playwright has no track record in the theater and he has no star who will sell tickets.

The press agent for the play, Seymour Krawitz, has a problem trying to drum up interest. He is counting heavily on me to give interviews to the press. I agree to do as much as I can between rewriting.

After the first few interviews I ran out of new things to say about my play. But I was expected to be funny, upbeat, and make people want to see the show. I'm not too sure I succeeded. Despite giving as many interviews as I could we still wound up with no sale.

The theater parties were not breaking down the box-office window. When word of mouth spread that we were in trouble in New Haven, we lost whatever hope we had of getting the people to buy tickets in advance of opening night.

Oscar Oleson, the general manager, says that if we're a hit and several other shows are flops, then we'll inherit their theater parties. Now I can understand why, despite all the goodwill in the world, people in the theater root for someone else's misfortune.

Here are some excerpts from interviews I gave:

With Mel Gussow of the New York *Times:*
"What have you learned from your theatrical experience?"

"I've learned, first, that it's a helluva way to break up a marriage. . . . Second. Never go to New Haven during Christmas week—for any reason. Third. You've written a play, you haven't written anything."

From a Myra McPherson interview in the Washington *Post:*
"I am preparing myself for defeat. Every second I'm not writing I'm preparing myself for all those things people are going to say if it doesn't work like 'I loved the set.' Or 'That line in the second act was tremendous.' I have made no plans for victory."

From the Wayne Robinson interview in the Philadelphia *Sunday Bulletin:*
"What have you learned about playwriting?"
"You eat lousy. You never eat a decent meal. I ate a hot dog the other night at Nathan's (my dinner) with three black muslims, two hippies from the Bronx, a taxi cab driver and a policeman, and we were all standing around the same table fighting over the same mustard."

From Daphne Kraft's interview in the Newark *Evening News:*
"Why did you write a play?"
"Male menopause. I just had to change my life and it was too late to have an affair and I don't drink."

With Bill Raidy of the Newhouse paper chain:
"Writing a play is like taking off all your clothes on Times Square."

From Tom Donnelly's interview in the Washington *News:*

"Most playwrights lose weight during the agonizing tryout period but Mr. Buchwald gained on the road. 'I felt sorry for myself so I ate a lot. I'd ask myself did I have a bad enough day to have cheesecake? Or Chinese food? I always did. The day I heard John McGiver was out of the play I ate a sixteen ounce steak, two baked potatoes, a salad and a piece of strawberry shortcake."

I never knew what a great sixteen-year-old son I had until the day I brought him to New York to see the show. In the afternoon he saw *Hair;* in the evening he saw *Sheep.* Without my pressing him, he said, "I liked your show better." It was the only nice thing anyone said to me all week.

January 16, 1970

Things are really going lousy. The cast seems to have lost interest in the play. They're walking through it. One night the audience likes it; the next night nothing happens. It's hard to figure what to fix because without Davey Burns we don't know what works and what doesn't. The ending is still unsatisfactory. The audience goes out of the theater perplexed.

I'm getting very sensitive to how people react to the play. If they come up to me after the play is over and say, "We love your column," I know they hated the show.

Gene is very concerned about when to open. He hasn't had a chance to invent new business because he's been so busy inserting the new material every afternoon. We've been cutting things that don't work, and the play is getting shorter and shorter. Most nights the audience is out in the streets by 10:25. Bob says not to worry. If they've had a good evening, they're happy to get out at 10.

A Few Thoughts About Theater Audiences

The price of tickets being what they are, the Broadway audiences for the most part are composed of upper-middle-class upper-middle-aged people. You rarely see young people at a Broadway show (with the exception of *Hair*). Off Broadway has more appeal to the young, and movies have more appeal than Off Broadway. At one time the theater was the place in America where you could say something that you couldn't say anywhere else.

This is no longer true. For the moment you can say anything you want in the United States, so you don't have to pay nine bucks to hear somebody else say it. Political satire in the theater works best in repressive society.

Besides, if that lady in Scarsdale decides, even after good reviews, that your play isn't her cup of tea, you can forget that summer home you were going to buy in Martha's Vineyard.

Laughs

One of the great mysteries of the theater is what happens to a laugh. For weeks we have been getting a big laugh on a line, and then suddenly one night no one laughs. We suspect it is just the way it was delivered, or perhaps the audience wasn't up for it. The next night the same thing happens. The laugh is gone. It left the theater. We do everything to bring it back again. But for some reason it refuses to return. Everyone is terribly shaken when this happens, particularly when no one has a reasonable explanation.

At the same time a line that for weeks has been laying an egg suddenly, for no reason, gets a laugh. It is not a particularly funny line, but the audience *wants* to laugh at it. Once again the actors are as perplexed as the director, producer, and author. What the hell's so funny, audience? How about letting us in on the joke?

If the laugh doesn't come out of character, it is called a cheap laugh. Bob and Gene are good about my not inserting any cheap laughs in the show. Our laughs are honest, clean, and upstanding. You would be proud to introduce them to your mother. I would have settled for less. Fortunately, Bob and Gene have more respect for the play.

Saturday, January 24, 1970

We've decided to open one week from tonight on January 31. Davey Burns goes in Monday. This means he will have less than one week to play the part. Gene doesn't believe it. Bob is nervous about any more postponements. Besides, it's cost him a fortune.

Roger Stevens has been magnificent through all our troubles. He has never shown he was discouraged. He even offered to put up more of his own money if necessary to get the show right. Whenever the rest of us have been down (which has been every night after the performance), he has insisted it's going to come out all right. I consider myself lucky to be involved with people who care more about the show than the money they've invested, which is now more than $200,000.

Roger and I have decided to have a blowout at Sardi's after the opening. We have 150 people coming up from Washington for the opening, none apparently Joe Alsop's friends.

SHAKESPEARE AT SARDI'S

I had a wild thought the other night. I wondered what would happen if William Shakespeare were writing for the theater on Broadway today. The mind boggles when you think of it.

The curtain has just rung down at the Globe Theater on Bill Shakespeare's latest play, *Romeo and Juliet,* and Shakespeare, clutching a fistful of congratulatory telegrams, stumbles over to Sardi's.

As he walks in, several people wave to him.

"It's a great play, Bill. I think you've got a hit."

"Jeez, Bill, how did you ever think of that plot? It's better than *West Side Story.*"

"Bill, dahling, Bill, dahling. What a sweet wonderful thing! If there was anything wrong with it, it was the director's fault."

"I watched Clive Barnes, Bill. He seemed to simply adore it. He was taking notes during the entire play."

"Bill, baby. Keep your fingers crossed. You could have a movie sale. I saw the gang from Paramount there tonight. We'll ask for two hundred and fifty thousand against ten percent of the gross. Of course, it all depends on Barnes. If the New York *Times* doesn't like it, you can kiss the movie sale good-bye."

"Here, Bill, have a drink. The television reviews won't be out for another twenty minutes. Frankly, I thought you could have cut some dialogue in the balcony, as it dragged a bit there. But on the whole, it held my attention."

"Billy, boy. It's one of your best. Of course, I'm not too sure how the audience is going to like the ending. It's a little downbeat for Broadway. I can see either the boy or the girl dying at the end, but why both of them?"

"Hey, Bill, the press agent has been looking for you."

"Hi, Bill. I heard someone say he heard Dick Watts of the *Post* say he liked it. . . . No, no word from Barnes. Relax, Bill, there's nothing you can do about it now."

"God knows you've written a lot more plays than I have, Bill, but how the hell did you ever let them cast that little girl as Juliet? She couldn't look more than fourteen years old. I liked the boy, though I thought the father should have been a little younger. But don't get me wrong —I liked it, Bill."

"Bill, Channel 5 is a rave. Stewart Klein said he hasn't seen anything like it in years. There's lots of good quotes. Now all we need is Ed Newman, Leonard Harris, and John Tucker. . . . What's that? WMCA hated it. Who gives a damn about WMCA?"

"Oppenheimer on *Newsday* just told a guy in Scarsdale who called a guy here, that as far as he's concerned, *Romeo and Juliet* is the best play he's seen all year."

"No word from Barnes."

"Barry Gray gave you a plug, Bill."

"Newman liked it! He had reservations about it, but on the whole, he liked it. You're in, Bill. Newman doesn't like many things."

"Here comes Leonard Lyons. Try to think of something funny that happened in Philadelphia."

"Hi, Leonard. You know Bill Shakespeare, don't you?"

"Good play, Bill. I was sitting with Justice William Douglas. He liked it, too."

"Someone was on the train with Walter Kerr and just called in. Kerr seemed to be arguing over the merits of the play with his wife. I don't know if he was for it and she was against it or if she was for it and he was against it."

"Kerr doesn't come out until Sunday."

"Bill, I didn't see the play, because we had to go to *Oh! Calcutta!,* but everyone at our table who saw it said they cried. It's hard to get people to cry in the theater anymore."

"Look—here comes Seymour. He's smiling. Barnes must have liked it."

"Barnes flipped over it. Listen to this: 'I must admit the idea of two teen-agers being in love with each other against the background of a family feud is something that ordinarily would set my teeth gnashing, but in the skillful hands of Bill Shakespeare, *Romeo and Juliet* is a play that I advise everyone to go and see....' "

"We're in, Bill! We're in!"

"Bless you, Bill. Next to Neil Simon, you're now the hottest playwright on Broadway."

The Log

Monday, January 26, 1970

Davey Burns went into the show tonight. He was unbelievable. Not only was the audience fascinated by his performance, but so was the cast. He broke up Marty Gabel and Liz Wilson on the stage. He got laughs where there were no laughs. But the rest of the actors lost their laughs because everyone was watching Burns.

It's amazing how one actor on the stage can change the balance of the play. But after the show the cast seemed to be delighted. Burns has breathed new life in the show. It is now much broader than it was before; but it works, and many lines that were laying there we've given to Davey.

Gene is worried and keeps asking for more time. He feels in two weeks Davey will be perfect (Burns doesn't know all his lines). Bob is afraid if we postpone once more, the critics will smell a herring and suspect we're in as much trouble as we really are.

I'm torn. I want the play to be right, but I also want the agony to be over with. I don't think I could stand another week of waiting for the ax to fall.

Tuesday, January 27, 1970

The decision has been made. We open Saturday come hell or the New York *Times*. I'm relieved.

The play is a spoof of many things, including the Pentagon. Tonight a man came up to me during intermission and said, "I'm Colonel Blank from the Pentagon, and I'd like to talk to you about your play."

"Oh, boy, here it comes," I said to myself.

The colonel continued very seriously: "The general in your play is wearing his combat badge on the wrong side of his chest."

"He is?"

"And the stripe on his pants is too narrow. And also the stripe on his sleeve."

"Is that all?"

"That's enough. Otherwise, I'm enjoying the play."

I went back to see Barnard Hughes, who plays the general, and said, "God damn it, Barney, if you can't wear your combat badge where it belongs, you can damn well get out of my show."

Thursday, January 29, 1970

Gene still wants to postpone. He blew up at the cast today during rehearsal. The nearer we get to opening night, the more nervous the actors are becoming. They're still asking what different lines mean. I can't believe they're serious. Margaret Ladd, the ingenue, cried today. She said Gene had been mean to her. I sat in the back of the theater with her and let her cry. I told her not to take it seriously, that the only thing that counted was opening night. Then I felt like crying.

We had a benefit audience tonight. I wasn't too thrilled with them either.

Friday, January 30, 1970

This was the night before the night that I've been waiting for. There is nothing more we can do. All of us would rather have one more month before we opened.

The big joke is: "Hey, the play is now ready to open in New Haven."

Now I have to devote all my thinking to Clive Barnes of the New York *Times*. I hope he doesn't have a fight with his wife tomorrow, and I hope his kids don't bug him and, God forbid he should have a mean taxi driver when he goes to the theater.

Please, Clive, like my show. Look, here are pictures of my kids. Would you pan a play written by someone with such nice-looking children? I don't want you to say you like the show if you don't—but at the same time don't lean over backward to be fair.

6. Opening Night

Saturday, January 31, 1970

This is it. I get up around eleven o'clock. Ann is going to the hairdresser's. People are coming in from Washington. My family in Forest Hills are more nervous than I am.

I don't have a damn thing to do. I'm told to stay away from the theater as it will do me absolutely no good. There is nothing I can do at this stage about anything. The party is in the hands of Jean Banquier and Vince Sardi. They've given us downstairs instead of upstairs. This is quite a deal, comparable to Diamond Jim Brady's taking over Sherry's.

I've seated every one of my friends and family in the first balcony. The seats cost me about $1,000. My share of the party's cost will be another $1,700. But I never had a Bar Mitzvah when I was a kid, and now I have a chance to make up for it.

I go up to Fifth Avenue and get a shine. Now that I've got the shine I *really* have nothing to do. I think I'll send telegrams to the cast. Better still, one telegram to the cast. I gave Gene, Bob, and Joe watches and Roger a plaque last night, so I can't even shop for gifts for them.

I walk up to Fifty-ninth Street. "Hello, New York.

I'm opening a play tonight. Over there on Broadway. If you all come and buy tickets, I'll be very happy."

Let's see, what would Gene Kelly do now? He'd dance on the fountain. Strike up the band, I want to sing and dance.

I think I'll go over to Broadway and see how my name reads on the marquee. There it is. All my life I've waited to see my name in lights on Broadway. And now a dream come true—I'm up there—squeezed between *Without a Stitch* and *I Am Curious—Yellow.*

What happened to the snow in New Haven, the lousy reviews in Philadelphia, the agony of rehearsal? It's all forgotten. This is where it's going to happen.

"Will you dig the show, New York?"

Okay, now let's go over to the GM Building. "Hello, everybody, this is your columnist turned playwright. Call me if you want house seats. I hope you want house seats. I hope the scalpers will be getting fifty dollars a pair. But don't worry, New York, you can have my seats at cost.

"You there, the pretty girl in the mini. If I write another show, I may have a part for you."

The Plaza. That's where I should go on the day my show opens. "I beg your pardon, you haven't seen Arthur Miller or Tennessee Williams walk through the lobby, have you?"

There are so many strangers from so many places in the Plaza. I wonder if they have a good ticket broker. "Hello, operator, give me information. Information, do you know what day this is? It's the greatest, most wonderful day of my life."

It's only three o'clock. If I could only get drunk.

Maybe I'll go by the theater just to see if my name is

spelled right on the marquee. "What do you mean? Who are you calling a ham?"

INVITATION

"The curtain for the opening night performance of *Sheep on the Runway* at the Helen Hayes Theater on Saturday evening, January 31, will rise at 7:45 P.M. sharp. Your promptness will be appreciated."

OPENING NIGHT BEFORE CURTAIN WENT UP

ME: "Hey, guess who I just took a leak with in the men's room? Walter Kerr."

Producers horrified!

"For Christ's sake. That was a stupid thing to do."

"It wasn't my fault. I was there first, and he came in. I couldn't very well stop."

"Dammit, now he'll feel compromised and will lean over backward to knock the show. Why didn't you pretend not to see him?"

"I did, but we were two urinals apart, and if I pretended to ignore him, he might have felt I was snubbing him."

"Oh, my God."

"It isn't as if I was passing him in the aisle or on the street. We were standing there facing the wall. I didn't say anything about the show."

"It doesn't make any difference. You embarrassed him by seeing him. Any experienced playwright would have zipped up and left immediately."

"Well, if it's that important, why don't they have johns for critics and johns for playwrights?"

"Because, except for someone like you, playwrights never go in the lounge before the play opens. You should have gone to Shubert Alley."

"Listen, I know Walter and Jean. I'm not sure, but I think I went to the men's room with him once in Paris. It won't affect the reviews."

"Oh, hell, it's too late now. We've lost Kerr—maybe Barnes will like it."

OPENING NIGHT

The best and most accurate description of what opening night was like was written by Mr. Paul Chaplin and appeared in the *Cavalier Daily,* the University of Virginia's newspaper in Charlottesville:

> On our recent trip to New York, Cavalier Daily drama critic Steve Wells and I decided to attend the premiere of Art Buchwald's new comedy, "Sheep on the Runway," in order to relate to you what the atmosphere of a Broadway opening night is like.
>
> As we walked east on 46th Street to the Helen Hayes Theatre, I could see two possible outcomes for the Buchwald play. It could be a surprise hit like the musical "1776" which is playing at the theatre next door, or it could fold quickly as did the one-night-bomb "La Strada," whose marquee was still up at the dark theatre across the street.

Advance word from the Philadelphia tryout as well
as Broadway rumors seemed to indicate the latter,
but I was optimistic.

We arrived outside the theatre ten minutes before the scheduled 7:45 curtain time, and were
forced to elbow our way through the mob of police,
celebrities, autograph seekers, photographers, and
curious bystanders to get inside. Delicately pushing
our way through the lobby, we eventually found
our seats in the mezzanine.

The theatre was filled with well-known person-
alities. Sitting around us were David Brinkley and
John Chancellor of NBC News, Jimmy Breslin, and
Vince Lombardi. Downstairs in the orchestra sat
Mayor and Mrs. John Lindsay, the Averell Harri-
mans, Ethel Kennedy, actresses Greer Garson and
Maureen Stapleton, and numerous New York and
Washington critics, columnists, and politicos.

The audience seemed quite content, despite a
fifteen minute delay. At eight o'clock the house
lights dimmed, the curtain went up and applause
greeted the set. Throughout the first act, the audience remained sharp and attentive, and rewarded
many lines in the play with applause and laughter.

Surprisingly, during the intermission, no one
seemed to have any opinions about the play. Jimmy
Breslin, however, was reportedly giving it three to
one odds of becoming a hit.

Something was different about the second act;
the audience seemed more at ease. Breslin was howl-
ing in his seat, and occasionally a loud guffaw could
be heard from the area where the NBC contingent
was sitting. The audience was very generous at the
play's conclusion, giving the cast three curtain calls,

with certain individuals crying, "Author! Author!"

Then came the long procession out of the theatre into the outside world—a mass of police, limousines, and the plain curious. Most everyone was smiling, but few comments were being made about the play. Everyone was more concerned with finding a way to get to Sardi's Restaurant, where co-producer Roger Stevens was hosting the post-premiere party. There they would anxiously wait to hear the opinions of the television critics. Steve, who is more familiar with New York critics than I, said it would be close.

The celebrities climbed into their limousines and drove off, while we walked the two blocks to the famous restaurant. I heard one theatre-goer remark, "Well, at least now we know Lindsay lives in New York," to be answered with "No, we now only know that Lindsay goes to the theatre in New York!"

After the crowd at the theatre, the small gathering at Sardi's was a relief, which unfortunately did not last. A mob sprung up as soon as the first car stopped outside the door. We quickly entered, checked our coats, and went to our table.

It was only a little after ten when we sat down; we would have an hour to wait for the first review. Suddenly, the entire floor broke into applause. I turned to see David Burns, the star of the show, enter the restaurant. He smiled and sat down, as a waiter brought forth an enormous blueberry cheesecake.

Occasional forced laughter interrupted the tense atmosphere, which increased as the minutes went by. The audience had reacted favorably towards Buchwald's first dramatic venture, but the fate of the play rested with the critics and their reviews.

At eleven o'clock, Steve and I began looking for a television so we could see the reviews. There was a five-inch screen Sony at the bar, but no one had bothered to turn it on.

A man at the bar turned around in surprise. "It's a dud! What do you think this is? The big event of the season?" I turned away only to confront a man with blond hair, round glasses, and a grey suit. "TV reviews don't mean a damn thing." This, I am told, is a misnomer. Television reviews are growing in importance with every new opening on Broadway. Furthermore, they usually serve as an indication of how the newspaper critics will respond.

A young woman in a black cocktail dress kept asking for someone to turn the TV on, and the bartender finally complied. NBC critic Edwin Newman appeared and silence surrounded the bar. His first remarks were discouraging. Upon hearing them the woman in black hissed, "Sh—!" Newman continued and his impressions became more favorable. He felt that despite the play's occasional silliness, it was at times very funny and pertinent. The general opinion of the elbow-benders at the bar was one of spirited satisfaction.

The bartender was told to change the channel to CBS for Leonard Harris' review. While waiting for it, we heard a burst of applause from the main dining room. Elizabeth Wilson, the female lead in the play, had just arrived. No sooner had we turned back to the TV, when the dining room once again applauded, more furiously than before. The recipient of this ovation was Mayor Lindsay. Once again, we returned to the miniature screen.

Finally, Harris appeared. The young woman quickly hushed everyone around the bar. The CBS critic gave a very favorable review, which included several quotes from the play. Although not exceedingly jubilant, the atmosphere around the bar was one of relief, with an element of surprise.

Steve and I walked around the restaurant to see how others had reacted. Oddly enough, everything was quiet, rather as if it were a normal night. Then we learned that few had heard the reviews as yet; we ourselves had only heard two of the four.

We went downstairs to discover Buchwald on the telephone. He repeatedly nodded his head, saying "yes" into the receiver. After he hung up, he walked around with a peculiar smile on his face, and addressing no one in particular, said out loud, "Four raves."

This was a slight exaggeration. While the reviews were all favorable, at least two of them were qualified. As no reviews would appear in the Sunday papers, these would have to suffice for the time being.

We went outside to inform our friend Tony, who has been doorman at Sardi's for twenty years and who had predicted an opening night disaster, that the reviews were favorable. He was as surprised as anybody, but felt final judgment rested with the papers. He added, "I hope it's a hit, 'cause we need a show on Broadway."

Returning to our table, we found ourselves relating excerpts of the reviews, which Steve had scribbled down on a cocktail napkin, to Will MacKenzie, another star in the show. He, like most everyone else, felt that the critics had been very fair.

We then talked to Dustin Hoffman's mother in "The Graduate," better known as Elizabeth Wilson. She was pleased with the reviews and hoped the play would be a hit because it had something important to say.

About 12:15, we prepared to leave Sardi's. At the entrance, Buchwald was saying goodnight to his father. He embraced him, saying, "I'll call you tomorrow, Papa." He was standing in a small group, with his trademark cigar in his hand, enjoying the whole event. We moved into the group and extended our congratulations to the new playwright. Steve asked him if the many rewrites were worth it, and he responded with a subtle but affirmative nod. We moved outside onto 44th Street, and headed uptown to keep another engagement.

Apparently the show had become a hit. Of course the papers were yet to judge, but there was a general feeling that those reviews would be equally kind, which they turned out to be, most especially Clive Barnes's notice in the New York Times. From all indications, "Sheep on the Runway" would not be typical of plays which experienced out-of-town difficulties.

It was about 2:30 A.M. when we last drove past the Helen Hayes Theatre. After midnight there is an eerie feeling that prevails over the Broadway theatre district. Except for a dim light in the lobby, the site of Buchwald's first theatrical triumph just a few hours before was now dark and silent. But, because the critics had reacted favorably, "Sheep on the Runway" in a few days would find its house crowded with ordinary New York theatre-goers, acting in the ritual of attending a hit play.

7. The Reviews

What a beautiful Bar Mitzvah party! Everyone who came seemed to like it. No matter what the critics say, I had a wonderful time. So did my father, my sisters, and my wife.

I learned something about the theater last night. If you start with a certain reputation, all you hope to do is come out of the experience with the same one you went in with. You ask for nothing more.

We spend the day walking along Fifth Avenue. There isn't much else to do. The Monday New York *Times* review won't be in until four in the afternoon. The *Daily News* about the same time. Dick Watts of the New York *Post* comes in later.

I go back to the Algonquin at three. Seymour has called. His wife spoke to Clive Barnes' wife. She reports Barnes liked it, but it won't be a rave. It sounds ominous. I sweat out a second call from Seymour. It comes through at four fifteen. Seymour is elated. He starts reading it on the phone. "Art Buchwald's 'Sheep on the Runway' is an always endearing, often very funny play." Then Barnes takes exception to the structure but continues: "However it remains a rattling good first play" and ends: "I wholeheartedly recommend 'Sheep on the Runway' warts and all. It may not be perfect but who is perfect?"

Good old Clive Barnes. He's a great man, a kind man, a truthful man.

May he live a long and happy life in the theater, and may he never have liver trouble on the road.

Douglas Watt of the *Daily News* likes it. Dick Watts of the New York *Post* likes it even more. Three out of the three newspapers in New York City give their blessing.

George Oppenheimer at *Newsday* gives it a rave. William Raidy of Newhouse papers hates it.

Both the AP's William Glover and the UPI's Jack Gaver aren't too thrilled with the play.

But for the moment the one that matters is Barnes.

If he likes it, you're in, and anything after that can help you. If he doesn't like it and the other critics do, it's all uphill.

(A week later Walter Kerr wrote his Sunday review, which was unfavorable, but by then we had a half-page ad quoting from the people who liked it, to counteract Kerr's pan.)

The *Wall Street Journal* didn't like the play. Martin Gottfried of *Women's Wear Daily* did. ("Don't worry, Art. People who buy tickets to Broadway pay more attention to *Women's Wear Daily*.")

I tried to be objective about the reviews. But it wasn't easy. The critics who gave the play good reviews, I decided, were brilliant writers filled with vision, depth, and understanding. They were able to see what I was trying to do, and I had nothing but admiration for their style, prose, and ability. The theater needed more like them.

The ones who disliked the play, for whatever reason,

I felt were lacking in humor and imagination and were probably frustrated playwrights themselves.

The theater would be a much better place without them.

There is no question who the good guys are.

George Oppenheimer in *Newsday:* "If it's laughter you want you can hardly do better than repair to the Helen Hayes Theater where Art Buchwald's 'Sheep on the Runway' opened Saturday night."

Richard Watts, Jr., of the New York *Post:* "It [*Sheep*] suffers from beginner's trouble with dramatic structure, but this weakness is more than atoned for by a steady flow of satirical hilarity."

Sandra Schmidt in the Los Angeles *Times:* "Well, it isn't quite a play. And it isn't a review, or really a satire or even a spoof. It is deathly murder as line by line each one-sided combatant mows himself down, adding another slash to his wrist everytime he opens his mouth, yet miraculously—and frighteningly—surviving to continue running the world."

Douglas Watt of the New York *Daily News:* "It is characterized by the same sharply funny and deceptively good natured approach that the writer customarily adopts toward the national scene."

Martin Gottfried in *Women's Wear Daily:* "Yet despite the drawbacks, the play is so pertinent so often that anyone at all aware of political America is bound to find it enormously intelligent and brutally ironic."

Leo Mishkin in the *Morning Telegraph:* "But in the end it's the Buchwald satire and the Buchwald jokes which will have you bellowing and chortling with delight."

Counting Sheep

Martin Nolan in the Boston *Globe:* "The only people who couldn't enjoy Buchwald's play are those who think the Viet Nam war was a swell idea."

Harry MacArthur in the Washington *Star:* "It's all pretty funny. It seems to have been a shock to New York, because apparently nobody has come up lately with just a genuinely funny play."

John Bartholomew Tucker of ABC TV: *"Sheep on the Runway* is a kind of political farce and Mr. Buchwald's brand of exaggeration for the sake of comedy turns into just about the funniest thing all year."

Variety: " 'Sheep' is thus a farce with a disquieting possibility of basic fact."

And now the bad guys.

NOTE—this list was dropped at the advice of all my friends in the theater just on the off chance I might be stupid enough to try to write another play.

The main thrust of the criticism from friend and foe alike was that the play lacked (a) plot; (b) construction; (c) a character with a rooting interest.

I could quarrel with that, but I could defend what we did on the grounds that had we had all the things the critics wanted, they would have probably beat my brains in.

Because of Barnes, I'm considered to have a hit. Everyone knows it. The people in the Algonquin, strangers who recognize me on the street. The secretaries of people I visit that day. I've received three calls from the William Morris Agency. The sweet smell of success is in the air, and I'm drinking in every minute of it.

I go to the advertising agency in the Sardi Building, where they're laying out the advertisements for the *Times,* the *News,* and the *Post,* telling the world that there is a new "laugh hit" on Broadway.

The selection of quotes by a critic to be used in an advertisement requires the talent of a surgeon. If the critic wrote, "I laughed in a few places," the press agent will drop the "in a few places" and will quote the critic as saying, "I laughed." I'm certain many critics have read quotes by themselves and have been very surprised to find they liked a play they hated.

So far the reviews break down to 75 percent favorable and 25 percent unfavorable. I'll settle for that anytime.

Roger Stevens says on the basis of the reviews we should run for at least a year, and with a movie sale I stand to make a quarter of a million dollars.

I have lunch with Joe Stein and thank him for everything he did. The most frustrating thing for a play doctor is to have worked on a play that turns out to be a hit and be unable to take the bows. If it's a bomb, the doctor doesn't want anyone to know he worked on the patient.

After lunch I go over to the Helen Hayes Theater to be interviewed by Leonard Probst of NBC. According to the lore of the theater, when you get very good reviews, there is supposed to be a line around the corner patiently waiting to get near the box office. Extra police are called out to see that the fans don't get disorderly.

When I got to the Helen Hayes, there were three people waiting in line. I ask the cashier how business is.

"Slow," he replies.

I gulp. How can this be? In the interview with Probst I complain about the lack of business, and that night at the theater everyone is furious with me. Seymour says, "What did you have to say a stupid thing like that for?"

THE NEXT TWO WEEKS

Despite the reviews, we're not doing the business we were supposed to do. Everyone is perplexed. The little lady in Scarsdale has decided she doesn't *have* to see our show. I say *have,* instead of "want," because Broadway depends on status-conscience people for its survival. There are certain shows that New York people *have* to see, just as there are certain books they *have* to read. If seeing your show is the thing to do, you can have a long and happy run. But if it doesn't matter whether they do or not, it's hard to survive.

The trick is to get off to a good start so tickets are very difficult to get. Then people will *have* to see your show because their neighbors couldn't get seats. Ticket brokers prefer "hard" ticket shows because then they can sell seats to it for a premium (illegal but the only way they can stay in business). No one in the theater complains when someone is scalping seats for his show because that means he's got a hit.

Unfortunately I never had the pleasure of seeing seats for *Sheep on the Runway* scalped.

The big problem for us is the nut, or what the show costs weekly to break even. Our nut is $31,000 a week, which is considered very high for a straight play. Our theater, if filled every night, can gross $59,000 a week. But it doesn't appear that we'll make that many weeks, if at all.

Some shows that run for eighteen months or two years and are considered hits do not play to large audiences, but their nut is low ($17,000 or $18,000 a week), and since the demand for theaters is not great, they can hang on.

But we have to get off with a bang. We have poured money into advertisements and radio spots. I've appeared on David Frost and Merv Griffin and been interviewed on a dozen radio shows plugging the play. But as *Variety* reported after the first two weeks, we look like a "nervous" hit. That means we can make it or we can't.

I've already kissed the $250,000 Roger said I'd make on the show good-bye.

I don't know what the future will bring, but yesterday, as I was leaving Washington for Manhattan, my wife said, "You see, aren't you glad you made them pay your expenses to New York?"

EPILOGUE

September 1, 1970

The show played 105 performances on Broadway, which was considered a good record. Only *Last of the Red Hot Lovers, Butterflies Are Free, Child's Play,* and *Borstal Boy* of the new plays last season had longer runs.

We took it to Washington for three weeks with the same cast and we had a tremendous reception, particularly since the play was so identified with this town. Then in June the original company disbanded.

The play will have a road company; there will be productions in London, France, and Germany, and it's been leased for stock and amateur rights.

So I can't consider all the time wasted.

When I look back on it, I consider my first experience in the theater worth every moment. Besides, Clive Barnes in his review said he hoped I'd write another play.

THE PLAY

Photo/Leo Friedman

THE SHEEP

Seated in front: WILL MACKENZIE, MARGARET LADD, Author ART BUCHWALD, MARTIN GABEL. Standing (left to right): Company Manager DAVID HEDGES, HELEN STENBORG, Master of Properties LIAM HERBERT (next to pole), BARNARD HUGHES, REMAK RAMSEY, Assistant Stage Manager BILL BECKER (with beard), ELIZABETH WILSON, NEIL FLANAGAN, EDA ZAHL, KURT GARFIELD (behind Miss Zahl), JEREMIAH MORRIS, DAVID BURNS, HENRY PROACH, Stage Manager HOWARD FISCHER, Director GENE SAKS, Master Electrician MICHAEL BURNS, SR., Press Representative SEYMOUR KRAWITZ, RICHARD CASTELLANO, Production Stage Manager FREDERIC DE WILDE, Producer ROBERT WHITEHEAD, Producer ROGER L. STEVENS.

Photo/Leo Friedman

Elizabeth Wilson and David Burns

Left to right: David Burns, Barnard Hughes, Neil Flanagan, Remak Ramsey, Richard Castellano, Martin Gabel (center)

Photo/Leo Friedman

Will Mackenzie
and Margaret Ladd

Remak Ramsey,
Barnard Hughes
and Jeremiah Morris
↓

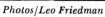
Photos/Leo Friedman

8. Sheep on the Runway

CHARACTERS

(In order of appearance)

AMBASSADOR RAYMOND WILKINS   David Burns
    United States Ambassador to Nonomura

MARTHA WILKINS   Elizabeth Wilson
    His Wife

SAM   Jeremiah Morris
    The Embassy's Loyal Servant

HOLLY   Margaret Ladd
    The Ambassador's Daughter

JOSEPH MAYFLOWER   Martin Gabel
    The Syndicated Political Columnist

FRED SLAYTON   Will Mackenzie
    Consul at the American Embassy

PRINCE GOW   Richard Castellano
    Ruler of Nonomura

GENERAL FITZHUGH   Barnard Hughes
    U.S. General in Charge of Military Aid

EDWARD SNELLING   Remak Ramsay
    U.S. Official in Charge of Civilian Aid

COLONEL NUM   Neil Flanagan

GUARDS AND WORKMEN   Kurt Garfield, Henry Proach

The entire play takes place in the living room of the United States embassy in the kingdom of Nonomura, a remote monarchy in the Himalayas

97

Synopsis of Scenes

ACT I

SCENE 1: A summer evening
SCENE 2: About a week later

ACT II

SCENE 1: The next morning
SCENE 2: Some time later

Act I

Scene 1   *The living room in the U.S. embassy in the kingdom of Nonomura, a remote monarchy in the Himalayas. It is a formal room with graceful columns, mostly Hindu in style. Upstage center are double doors leading to a hallway which serves other parts of the building as well as the front door of the embassy. Stage left are doors leading to a dining room, and upstage right is a door leading to a study or workroom. There is an outdoor balcony downstage right from which one can view the town and the surrounding mountains.*

Furnishings in the room include an Oriental coffee table centerstage with three-tiered pillow seats right and left of table and a small black stool upstage center. There is a pot of orchids on the table with an ashtray and cigarette lighter. On the stage-right wall there is a large cabinet-desk on which is a telephone. On a small stand downstage of desk is a shortwave radio receiver. There is a bar downstage left of dining room door with the seal of the American embassy on it. On the wall are framed photographs of

> *President Nixon and Vice President Agnew.*
> *Agnew's photo is slightly crooked.*
> *Before the curtain rises, we hear radio*
> *voices in Russian, Chinese, Spanish, etc.*
> *The curtain goes up and we see* AMBAS-
> SADOR RAYMOND WILKINS *dressed in black*
> *tie and white smoking jacket struggling*
> *with the dials.*

RAYMOND

God damn the Voice of America!

> (*Calls offstage*)

Martha, what the hell band is the Voice of America, again?

> (*No answer. He goes back to fiddling with*
> *the dials*)

VOICE OF AMERICA

... who denied any wrongdoing, although he admitted taking the money. . . . This is the Voice of America signing off in English for tonight. Tomorrow our program will be devoted to the American TV dinner and how it changed the eating habits of the free world.

> (RAYMOND *turns off radio in disgust as*
> MARTHA WILKINS, *his wife, enters in fetch-*
> *ing gown*)

MARTHA

Any news tonight?

RAYMOND

All I heard this time was that someone in Congress denied any wrongdoing, although he admitted taking the money.

MARTHA

Oh? I hope it isn't anybody we know.

RAYMOND

God, we're isolated out here.

MARTHA

(*Looks at Nixon and Agnew*)

After all the money you raised for them—the least they could have done for you was give you a decent embassy.

(*Straightens Agnew's picture*)

RAYMOND

Is Joe still unpacking? He's the most prissy newspaperman I know. He brought his own bottled water and lily cups. Says he never takes chances in a foreign country. God, I hope he likes his room.

MARTHA

Stop being so nervous, Raymond. Why wouldn't he like his room?

RAYMOND

Because if Joe's unhappy, he can be a mean son of a bitch.

MARTHA

Well, maybe you shouldn't have invited him.

RAYMOND

I didn't invite him. He invited himself. Seemed like a

101

good idea to me at the time. I thought at least he'll write some columns and people will know where we are.

MARTHA
Raymond, I want you to show him those plans you've drawn up.

RAYMOND
I don't know. He might think I'm being pushy.

MARTHA
Well, I'm going to show them to him the first chance I get. You're always too modest.

RAYMOND
Use your own judgment. I hope he hits it off with the Prince.

MARTHA
Well, of course, he'll hit it off with the Prince. Joe adores royalty. Sam, no orchids on coffee table. You understand ... no orchids here. Your Prince is coming to dinner tonight. You understand. Everything must be perfect. We don't have enough orchids. I knew I should have gotten more orchids. I hope this protocol book is up to date. Now, when dinner is announced, who enters the dining room first? The Prince? The Prince and me? Me and you? You and the Prince? The Prince and Joe? And who sits down first?

RAYMOND
The Prince goes first and sits first.

MARTHA

And after dinner the head of state and the ambassador exchange toasts. Raymond, do you have the toast?

RAYMOND

I've been trying to memorize it all day. Here, see if I've got it right. Your Highness, Kipling once said "East is East and West is West and never the twain shall meet." Well, Kipling was a liar and we're proving it here tonight. Furthermore . . .

MARTHA

Raymond, do you think you should call Kipling a liar?

RAYMOND

Why not? He's dead. Besides, I think the Prince will like that. Furthermore, I wish to say I hope the people of Nonomura and the U.S. will always remain friends.

MARTHA

Well, they're certainly far enough away from each other to remain friends.

RAYMOND

Long live the Prince! There, that does it.

MARTHA

But I don't know what to talk about.

RAYMOND

Let Joe steer the conversation. It's his evening.

MARTHA

It's the first time the Prince has come to the embassy and I am so afraid of making a gaffe.

RAYMOND

Goddammit, Martha, you're making me nervous. It's bad enough worrying about Joe without having to worry about you.

MARTHA

I can't help being nervous. I don't even know if the Prince eats meat loaf.

RAYMOND

Meat loaf. Good God, you're not serving the Prince meat loaf?

MARTHA

It happens to be our President's favorite dish.

RAYMOND

Well, I didn't know that. Here's some mail for you that came in on the plane with Joe.

MARTHA

Lord and Taylor's, Saks Fifth Avenue, Tiffany's, Garfinckel's . . .

RAYMOND

How come the State Department doesn't know where we are, but every department store in the United States can find us?

MARTHA

Here's a letter from Isobel Stone . . . I'm not going to walk around in rags just because we're living in outer space . . . the Agnews gave a dinner party for Miss America . . . the best parties in Washington are now being given by the

Ethiopians . . . and David Eisenhower and Julie have just
come out against pot.

RAYMOND

God, I thought it was dull out here.

MARTHA

Oh, by the way, Raymond. Holly refuses to come down
for dinner.

RAYMOND

(Angry)

Why?

MARTHA

She said we had no right to make her come here for her
summer vacation.

RAYMOND

No right? We're her parents. Just because she's had a
year at college doesn't give her a right to tell us we have
no rights.

(Goes to door and shouts offstage)

Holly—Holly, get your tail down here right away.

(To MARTHA)

We're going to lay down a few rules right now.

(Door offstage slams)

MARTHA

I told you we should have sent her to a Catholic school.

> (HOLLY *enters wearing Radcliffe sweat
> shirt, skirt, and is barefoot. She looks as if
> she's been crying)*

RAYMOND
Holly, why aren't you dressed for dinner?

HOLLY
I don't want to eat.

RAYMOND
The Prince is coming for dinner and you're damn well going to eat with us.

HOLLY
I told you I wanted to stay home this summer.

MARTHA
But, Holly, we haven't seen you in six months. Surely, you can give your parents two months out of your life.

RAYMOND
What were you planning to do at home that was so important?

HOLLY
You wouldn't understand it, if I told you.

RAYMOND
Look, I don't know what you're doing these days, young lady, but because of whatever you were up to at Radcliffe, I almost didn't get my security clearance.

HOLLY
I'm sorry you did. It screwed up everything for me.

MARTHA
Don't talk that way to your father.

RAYMOND

Now let's get something straight. At this moment, you are the daughter of His Excellency, the Ambassador of the United States. You will do nothing—do you hear me?—nothing, to embarrass your mother or me. Prince Gow is coming to dinner tonight and you will be so charming he won't be able to stand it.

HOLLY

And what if I'm not?

RAYMOND

Then you will not go back to Radcliffe in the fall. You will stay here with us as long as *we*'re here.

HOLLY

I might have known you'd think up something dirty like that.

MARTHA

Holly, change for dinner.

(HOLLY exits)

RAYMOND

(*Yelling off to her*)

... And remember, you better be charming.

MARTHA

... Yes, please be charming ...

RAYMOND

(*Goes to door*)

And put on some shoes, goddammit.

> (*To* MARTHA)
> I worked all my life, made a fortune so my daughter could run around without shoes on.

MARTHA
Isobel's daughter's worse. She's living in Georgetown with a rock group called The Blood Transfusions.

> (JOE *enters, looks around, goes to Agnew and Nixon pictures ... peers behind them*)

RAYMOND
What's up, Joe?

JOE
I'm looking for the microphones ... the bugs. In the Thailand embassy, they found it behind Agnew, but since then I heard they're putting it behind Nixon ...

RAYMOND
Oh, no, this is a quiet country. They wouldn't go to the trouble to ...

JOE
They'd do anything ... anything ...

> (*He continues searching around room during the following dialogue*)

RAYMOND
What you need is a drink, Joe. Do you see that savage over there? Can't speak a word of English and only understands two words: vodka martini. And I taught him. Sam, two vodka martinis, please.

JOE
(*To* RAYMOND)
Wait a minute—I want to test him.

(*To* SAM)
Make mine with Beefeater gin. Martini with Beefeater.

(*To* RAYMOND)
If he understands me, we're in trouble.

(*To* MARTHA)
Well, how have you been, Martha?

MARTHA
(*Looking at* SAM)
Fine; I've been fine.

JOE
And you, Raymond; how have you been?

RAYMOND
Me too, I've been fine, too . . . How about you, Joe?

JOE
Fine, I'm fine . . . fine . . .

(JOE *sips his drink. They watch anxiously*)

It's a vodka . . . He's OK.

(*Up to* SAM)

Very good . . . very good Beefeater martini.
Can't be too careful. Now, Raymond, did you round up
those Red Chinese refugees for me?

RAYMOND

Still working on it, Joe. They aren't as easy to come by as I thought, but I'm sure we'll find some.

JOE

Don't fail me now. I always do a Red Chinese refugee column when I come to this part of the world.

(*Finds wire under steps. Triumphantly he says*)

Got it!

(*Pulls wire ... lamp falls over*)

Sorry.

MARTHA

(*Picks up lamp*)

That's all right, Joe ... Raymond, tell him about your idea. I think it would make a good column, Joe.

(*She hands plan to* RAYMOND, *who is slightly embarrassed*)

RAYMOND

Look at this, Joe. It's my own plan for developing Nonomura. We could make this the tourist mecca of Asia.

MARTHA

Raymond has worked so hard on this.

RAYMOND

You see, it's a gigantic year-round resort ... I'm going to call it the Shangri-La Town and Country Club ...

MARTHA

The President knew what he was doing when he sent Washington's biggest builder to Nonomura.

JOE

Very interesting, but I came to this part of the world to take the political temperature. What is it?

RAYMOND

All right, I guess.

JOE

All right. What do you mean, all right?

MARTHA

One day blends right into the next.

RAYMOND

Very quiet, Joe. We couldn't even get the Yale Glee Club, who were in Bombay, to come up here. And they'll sing anywhere.

JOE

What have you done to persuade the Prince to join the Western camp?

RAYMOND

Oh, I've been working on that, Joe. We send over American movies to the palace every week. They're the Prince's favorite, next to the Swedish ones.

JOE

I don't mean movies, Raymond. Is he committed to the free world?

RAYMOND

By God, I'm glad you asked me that.

JOE

Well, is he?

RAYMOND

I'm going to ask him that.

JOE

What's he like?

RAYMOND

Peach of a guy, Joe. Plays poker, goes tiger hunting, and chases women—not necessarily in that order.

JOE

Married?

RAYMOND

His wife died a tragic death a few years ago. She was bowing to him and had a concussion when she hit her head too hard on the floor.

MARTHA

But he's not unhappy, Joe. He has a stable of concubines, and when he gets bored, the French ambassador presents him with the most extraordinary girls from Paris.

JOE

Remember, Raymond, I've got to talk to the Prince alone.

RAYMOND

It's all arranged. After dinner, we'll have coffee in the dining room and leave you two alone. What do you want to talk to him about?

JOE

I want to know what's going on here.

RAYMOND

Nothing really, Joe . . . I told you . . .

JOE

I mean underneath, Raymond—underneath where the turmoil is; where the real trouble is.

RAYMOND

What trouble?

JOE

You're too close to it, Raymond. I feel it . . . this place is boiling.

RAYMOND

It is?

JOE

Boiling.

MARTHA

You never stop working, do you, Joe?

JOE

I'd love to, Martha, but I'll only stop working when the world stops spinning. You know, I've been to four countries in three days. I saw Chiang Kai-shek in Formosa. He looks fit. He still wants to have a go at the mainland.

RAYMOND

Oh.

113

Counting Sheep

JOE

I told him to hold off. Do you realize the average age of one of Chiang Kai-shek's privates is now sixty-four? Then I came over to New Delhi to have a chat with Madame Pandit. While I was there, it occurred to me that you and Martha were up here, and since I hadn't done a column yet on the Commie threat to small, neutral nations, I decided to come up and visit you. My God, Raymond, what a sunset!

RAYMOND

Yep, it's a great spot if you like to look at the sun go down.

MARTHA

Those are the Himalayas out there. I don't believe there's a view like this in all the world. Raymond put a picture window in the dining room.

RAYMOND

I put in a requisition to Washington for a big pane of glass, and they turned me down. Damned bureaucrats.

MARTHA

Smell that air, Joe.

RAYMOND

You don't find air like that in the United States anymore. There's a lot to be said for a country that's still in the nineteenth century.

MARTHA

There's the Prince's palace . . . There's the university, and . . . Raymond, the flag!

RAYMOND

I'll take it down.

MARTHA

No, you stay with Joe. I'll take it down.

(*She exits*)

JOE

You have to take down the flag yourself?

RAYMOND

Either Martha or I do it—most embassies rate a Marine color guard, we don't even get a Wac. But you know something? The natives are very impressed. They come out and watch. And we've started something here. Now every ambassador has to take down his flag. But Martha still gets the biggest crowds . . . See them down there . . .

JOE

She's a fine American.

RAYMOND

There she goes.

(*Hand over heart*)

And Martha's doing a wonderful job here, Joe. Not only with the flag. She's president of the American Nonomuran Friendship Club, she's secretary of the Diplomatic Wives' Circle, and she's started a Birth Control Society.

JOE

Old Glory couldn't be in better hands.

(FRED *enters*)

RAYMOND

Ah, Fred.

FRED

Good evening, Mr. Ambassador.

RAYMOND

Fred, this is the notorious and widely syndicated columnist Joseph Mayflower.

FRED

We're honored.

RAYMOND

Joe, this is Fred Slayton, my Number One. Been here for
four years, knows the country from one end to the other,
and actually speaks the language.

FRED

I didn't think Nonomura would have any attraction for
someone like you, Mr. Mayflower.

RAYMOND

We were just discussing the political situation here, Fred.

FRED

I'm afraid you'll find it rather dormant, Mr. Mayflower.
Nothing much happening.

RAYMOND

I wouldn't say that. I feel that underneath the surface . . .
where the turmoil is . . . this place is boiling.

FRED

But, Mr. Ambassador, nothing at all is going on up here.

JOE

I would listen to the ambassador, young man. He'd know if anything is going on.

FRED

What? What? Where is it boiling?

RAYMOND

Where is it boiling? . . . Tell him, Joe.

JOE

Does the name General Hung Kai mean anything to you?

FRED

I don't think there's much there, Mr. Mayflower. He's a bandit chieftain up north. His family has controlled that area for two hundred years.

JOE

How does the Prince feel about him?

FRED

Well, he doesn't much care one way or the other. They have a gentleman's agreement that if Kai stays out of the south, the Prince will stay out of the north. They probably have a joint bank account in Switzerland.

JOE

My sources in New Delhi seem to think he's a Communist.

FRED

I wouldn't believe everything I heard in New Delhi.

117

JOE

Oh, you wouldn't?

FRED

Well . . .

JOE

Are you trying to tell me what to believe and what not to believe in New Delhi?

FRED

No, sir, that's not what I mean . . . It's just that I don't see any Communist threat here.

JOE

And what threats have you seen? How many threats have you seen? I've seen threats where nobody else has seen them. I've been to places where they tell me no threat, no threat—and I said there is a threat, and by God there was a threat. Sometimes a little threat, sometimes a big threat, but always a threat.

FRED

But to the best of my knowledge.

JOE

Knowledge . . . knowledge . . . It can ruin you. Let me tell you something, young man. There's only one thing I depend on . . . my sixth sense—smell. I smell something here, and I don't like it.

(MARTHA *comes in with* HOLLY)

MARTHA

Oh, hello, Fred.

FRED

Hello, Mrs. Wilkins.

RAYMOND

Holly, this is Fred Slayton, my Number One.

HOLLY

Daddy wrote me about you. He said you keep the embassy from falling apart.

MARTHA

And you were on the plane with Joe. You must have had a nice chat.

HOLLY

But we didn't chat.

MARTHA

Why not?

HOLLY

I was vomiting.

MARTHA

Holly, for heaven's sakes!

HOLLY

Well, I didn't plan it, Mother. It just happened.

JOE

I'd never have recognized her. I haven't seen her in seven years.

HOLLY

Ah, but I've seen you, Mr. Mayflower. I was one of the students who walked out on you at Harvard when you gave us all that garbage about Vietnam.

RAYMOND
Holly, that's no way to talk to Mr. Mayflower.

JOE
Holly is being duped along with hundreds of thousands of other university students by a worldwide Communist plot. They're not even aware of it.

HOLLY
You'd like to think that, don't you, Mr. Mayflower? If it's a worldwide Communist plot, it makes things very convenient for you.

RAYMOND
What the hell does that mean?

HOLLY
In that way you don't have to try to find out how the students really feel about the war or all the other things we're against.

JOE
All I know is that what the students are doing in the United States brings elation to Moscow.

HOLLY
And all I know is you worry too much about what the Russians are thinking and not enough about what the American students are thinking.

MARTHA
Holly, a year of college doesn't give you the right to talk to Mr. Mayflower that way.

HOLLY

I'm terribly sorry, Mother. Mr. Mayflower, I would have been delighted to have chatted with you on the plane, if I hadn't been vomiting.

RAYMOND

Fred, Holly believes she made a mistake coming here this summer.

FRED

I would think anyone would jump at the chance to come to Nonomura.

HOLLY

You would?

FRED

You may be in for a big surprise, Holly. This is a beautiful country. We have rain forests, fantastic birds and fauna, and monkeys, tigers, and Mount Shima, which is called the Diamond of the Himalayas.

HOLLY

It sounds great, but I've got to be where it's happening. And it's not happening here.

FRED

What do you mean, where it's happening?

HOLLY

Whatever you're doing here isn't relevant. I wanted to do something relevant this summer.

FRED

What would you have done back in the States?

Counting Sheep

HOLLY

You really want to know?

FRED

Yes, I do.

HOLLY

I was going to organize the girls at Gimbels to join the student revolution and overthrow the system.

MARTHA

You mean, our system?

JOE

That's exactly what she means.

FRED

Well, we don't have a Gimbels here, so I guess you won't have anything to organize.

RAYMOND

Maybe I'll build her a shopping center.

HOLLY

Well, here's to the summer. Say, where's the Prince? I hear he's sexy.

FRED

I'm sure he'll like you.

HOLLY

Maybe I could seduce him ... for the United States, of course. Father, would you like me to seduce the Prince and find out his state secrets?

122

RAYMOND
Now knock off that kind of talk, Holly. It's not very funny.

FRED
You can't seduce the Prince anyway. It's against protocol.
He has to seduce you.

MARTHA
I've never heard anything like it. My own daughter.

JOE
It's everybody's own daughter, Martha.

(*Sound of horns*)

RAYMOND
That's him. That's the Prince.

FRED
There's the Prince now.

MARTHA
I thought you told me he was coming alone.

FRED
He is, Mrs. Wilkins, but he never leaves the palace without his bodyguards.

JOE
He has a Silver Cloud Rolls-Royce.

RAYMOND
I told you, he lives well. Sam, get the door.

JOE
He puts on a good show.

HOLLY

What do I do? Do I curtsy?

RAYMOND

No, you bow. Hands clasped as in prayer, bend from the waist to a sharp forty-five-degree angle. Don't they teach you anything at Radcliffe?

FRED

His Royal Highness, Prince Salong Gow, Exalted Ruler of the Kingdom of Nonomura.

PRINCE

Forgive me for being late. There was a constitutional crisis.

RAYMOND

A constitutional crisis?

PRINCE

The people wanted a constitution. I keep pointing out to them that countries that have a constitution have a great deal more trouble than those who do not.

RAYMOND

You have a point, Your Highness.

PRINCE

It's very disconcerting. Someone is stirring up my country. But I do not mean to inflict my problems on you. Mrs. Wilkins, I am most honored that you should receive me in your embassy. May I present you with a small token of my gratitude?

MARTHA

Oh, Your Highness. It's beautiful.

PRINCE

It is a replica of the Princess HuRani, who is revered in my country as the Goddess of Beautiful Women.

MARTHA

You do me honor.

PRINCE

And for you, Mr. Ambassador,

(*Takes a large medal off another pillow*)

for what you have done for Nonomura, I have the honor to make you a Royal Chevalier of the Order of the Golden Elephant.

(*Places medal around* RAYMOND's *neck*)

RAYMOND

Your Highness, I am overwhelmed.

MARTHA

Oh, Raymond. It's beautiful.

RAYMOND

So's yours. And now, Your Highness, Mrs. Wilkins and I have a little gift for you.

PRINCE

Oh, thank you!

MARTHA

No, Your Highness, that's our daughter. Raymond, have you got it?

(RAYMOND *goes to desk, looks for present, finally gives* MARTHA *a nod.* MARTHA *goes to desk and looks*)

Sam.

(SAM *goes to desk and gets photograph and gives it to* RAYMOND)

RAYMOND
It's a signed photograph of our President and his wife.

PRINCE
"To His Royal Highness, Prince Gow, with fondest affections. Pat and Dick." Which is Pat? Which is Dick?

RAYMOND
This is the President of the United States, and this is the First Lady.

PRINCE
I shall cherish it forever.

MARTHA
Your Highness, this is the world-famous syndicated columnist Joseph Mayflower.

PRINCE
Ah, Mr. Mayflower. I am truly honored. I have read many of your columns, as well as your book *The Many Roads to War*.

JOE
Your Highness, please accept this autographed copy of my latest book.

126

PRINCE
Thank you very much. *Is Peace Inevitable?* I shall read it tonight. The ambassador informs me that you wish to interview me on the world situation. I am most flattered that you would come here to seek out my opinions.

JOE
Your Highness, it is I who is honored that you should agree to see me. The winds of the cold war know no boundaries, and what you have to say concerns my readers as much as the opinions of the mightiest nations.

PRINCE
You must stay for a while and visit the whole of my country.

JOE
Would that I could. That's John Gunther's bag.

RAYMOND
Your Highness, this is my daughter, Holly. She goes to school in America . . . Radcliffe.

HOLLY
I am charmed, absolutely charmed.

PRINCE
Ah, Mr. Ambassador, you did not tell me that you had such a beautiful daughter. I have heard of Radcliffe.

HOLLY
And we at Radcliffe have heard of you. I was so thrilled when my father was posted here, because all my life, my one desire above everything else has been to come to Nonomura.

PRINCE

How delightful! Tomorrow you will come to the palace, if you like, and we will have some tea, and perhaps you will tell me what the American students are thinking.

HOLLY

What a marvelous idea.

PRINCE

We have a beautiful university here, you know, but unfortunately the students are becoming restless. The education has gone to their heads. Perhaps someone like you could convince them of the error of their ways.

HOLLY

I'd certainly like to try.

FRED

Jesus!

PRINCE

Do you like tiger hunting, my child?

HOLLY

Adore it. That's all we ever talked about in the dorm.

PRINCE

Then by all means, we must have a tiger hunt in your honor.

(SAM *rings gong*)

MARTHA

Shall we go in to dinner?

PRINCE

I have read recently where the King of Nepal has been invited to Washington on a state visit, is that so?

FRED

Yes, it is, Your Highness. We're working on that for you.

PRINCE

I should have thought I would have been invited before the King of Nepal.

RAYMOND

It's probably done alphabetically, Your Highness. Well, I'm starved.

PRINCE

You know, Mr. Mayflower, I've never been invited to Washington. It does seem rather odd.

JOE

We'll have to do something about that then, won't we?

PRINCE

Of course, I realize that we are a small country.

FRED

Believe me, Your Highness, size has nothing to do with it.

PRINCE

You know my family dynasty does go back some five hundred years before the King of Nepal's. You would have thought that they would have taken that into consideration.

JOE

There are more important things to consider, Your Highness.

PRINCE

But the King of Nepal . . .

JOE

Forget about the King of Nepal. I'm talking about what is happening in this area.

RAYMOND

After Joe's interview with you, I'm sure your name will become as well known as the King of Nepal's . . .

MARTHA

Will you gentlemen stop talking business? The dinner is getting cold. Your Highness, you sit on my right, and, Joe, you are on my left.

> (*During this exiting,* SAM *comes in from office, takes a paper from desk, pins it on post, and takes a flash picture with Minox camera. Then picks up glasses as lights dim. The lights come up immediately as* PRINCE *and* JOE *enter from dining room*)

PRINCE

I have nothing personal against the King of Nepal. I will admit that he is the king of kings, five times godly, the divine emperor, and possibly, as he claims, the incarnation of the Hindu god Vishnu, but I just can't see him eating meat loaf at the White House.

JOE

I understand how you feel, Your Highness, but the United States happens to be interested in the King of Nepal.

PRINCE

Why? Why him?

JOE

Because the Russians are interested in him, and the Chinese are interested in him, and the French are interested in him, and the British used to be interested in him when they were interested in anything.

PRINCE

And no one is interested in me?

JOE

Your Highness, meaning no disrespect, your country is at best a source of amusement to the world.

PRINCE

You don't mean it ...

JOE

You are considered an underdeveloped nation by under-developed nations ...

PRINCE

But we are members in good standing of the UN.

JOE

Yes, and do you know that when your delegate talks, there is no simultaneous translation.

PRINCE

Nobody listens?

JOE

Nobody is there. They schedule him to speak at six o'clock in the morning.

PRINCE

Why? Why are we treated this way?

JOE

Because you persist in this absurd fiction that your country is impervious to the forces that are shaking the earth, the forces of light and darkness. You persist in the fiction that these forces do not affect your people, that you can avoid the responsibilities of life in this century, the responsibility of taking a position, of aligning yourself with one or another of the great power blocs, of using your strategic location for good or ill, or walking the dangerous tightrope of neutrality over the abyss that we call civilization.

PRINCE

Everyone tells me that.

JOE

You are not listening, Your Highness. You're not listening to me.

PRINCE

I'll listen, I'll listen. What?

JOE

Your country can only attain greatness when it recognizes the reality of world forces, the existence of its enemies, enemies within and without.

PRINCE

What enemies?

JOE

General Hung Kai for one.

PRINCE

Oh, him. He's avaricious and unscrupulous and selfish and traitorous, but I trust him.

JOE

My information is that he is backed by the Communists.

PRINCE

Impossible. He's far too wealthy.

JOE

And if he is, there is no reason why our country shouldn't come to your assistance . . .

(PRINCE *shakes his head*)

with token help, and no obligations . . . unless you are forced to use this assistance against your Communist-supported enemies in the north . . .

(PRINCE *shakes his head*)

to repel this threat against your sovereignty . . . stop shaking your head at me. I've come halfway around the world to see you. I could have been with Pompidou. I could have been with Tito. I come here to tell you there's a threat to your little country and you keep shaking your head at me. I won't have it. There are people all over the world begging me for the benefit of my wisdom and

my advice. And, you sit there and shake your head at me.
Charles de Gaulle never shook his head at me. Lyndon
Johnson never shook his head at me. No one has ever
done that to me.

PRINCE

Please, Mr. Mayflower.

JOE

No one!

PRINCE

Mr. Mayflower.

JOE

Ever!

PRINCE

Please, please, Mr. Mayflower. All right, all right. What
do you want me to say?

JOE

I want you to recognize that there is a threat out there.

PRINCE

All right, all right, there's a threat, there's a threat.

JOE

(*Calm and dignified*)

That's very interesting, Your Highness. Though it doesn't
surprise me.

(*Takes out pad*)

When did you first become aware of this danger?

The Play

PRINCE

Well . . . how about . . . last Wednesday?

(Moon Dragon Festival starts)

JOE

What's that?

PRINCE

The holiday's begun.

JOE

What holiday?

PRINCE

The Festival of the Moon Dragons.

*(HOLLY, FRED, MARTHA, RAYMOND enter
from dining room)*

HOLLY

What's happening?

FRED

It's the Festival of the Moon Dragons.

MARTHA

Oh, lovely.

RAYMOND

Joe, this country has more goddamn festivals than you
can shake a stick at.

MARTHA

Look at the beautiful flowers.

135

HOLLY

Look at the dragon masks.

(SAM *passes out lighted sparklers*)

MARTHA

Did everyone get a sparkler? Your Highness? Your Highness, what is the significance of it?

PRINCE

It honors the maidens of Nonomura. The maidens have a battle of orchids. They throw them at the unmarried men.

HOLLY

How long has this been going on?

PRINCE

For over six hundred years. You must throw an orchid. Here, my child. Because you are a virgin.

HOLLY

(*Hesitates, then throws orchid into audience*)

May the Moon Dragon forgive me.

(Blackout.
In the blackout, we hear the VOICE OF AMERICA *saying . . .*)

Act I

Scene 2   *The embassy living room. About a week*
             later.
             In the dark we hear the VOICE OF AMERICA.

VOICE OF AMERICA

. . . and the press secretary
stated that the President
was aware of the tense situation in Nonomura and
added, "The President
wants to make it perfectly
clear that the United States
will not stand idly by and
see the freedom-loving
people of Nonomura fall to
Communist aggression."

                              FRED
                              (*Enters, picks up ringing
                              phone*)

The President is following   Hello, hello. No, Mr.
the situation closely and   Mayflower is not here. I
has ordered the Joint Chiefs   don't know where he is.
of Staff to keep him per-   (*Hangs up*)
sonally informed of   Mr. Ambassador! Mr.
developments.   Ambassador . . .

                                        137

The President also an-
nounced that he was going
to Key Biscayne   . . . Mr. Ambassador . . .
for the weekend.   (*Answers phone again*)

In Congress, members   No, I'm sorry. Anything
raised questions about the   the ambassador says now
Nonomuran situation,   could jeopardize hopes for
several asking why   peace. Mr. Ambassador!
Congress needed to learn   (FRED *exits*)
of the Nonomuran threat
through the newspapers.

The Senate Foreign
Relations Committee
planned to call the
Secretary of State for
hearings.   (RAYMOND *enters*)

VOICE OF AMERICA
Mr. Raymond Wilkins, American Ambassador to Nonomura, was quoted as saying . . .

(*Static, static, static*)
. . . without first talking to Ambassador Wilkins.

RAYMOND
What? What without first talking to me?

VOICE OF AMERICA
The Long Island Railroad announced today it was dis-
continuing passenger service.

(RAYMOND *turns off radio.* FRED *enters*)

FRED

Read these, sir. We're getting a communications team that will plug into the war room at the White House. Army, Navy, and Air Force military attachés, a defense intelligence coordinator, and an independent study group from the University of Michigan.

RAYMOND

Where the devil are we going to put all these people?

FRED

We shouldn't have let Joe start his war before we got the Shangri-La Town and Country Club built.

RAYMOND

That's unfair, Fred. There's no war. Nothing's changed around here except that Washington's finally acknowledged our existence.

FRED

It took Mayflower only one lousy week to turn this place upside down. I'll give him credit for one thing. His column does have readership. Peking's holding a rally in support of General Hung Kai.

RAYMOND

Then there must have been something to Joe's claim that Hung Kai was a Communist. Even if he wasn't one.

FRED

He wasn't one before, but he's one now, whether he wants to be or not. Four years' work down the drain.

(Phone rings again. FRED *picks it up)*

Wa-shu. What? . . . No, not yet. Thank him very much, but tell him it's too early. Jesus.

RAYMOND

Who was that?

FRED

It was Bob Hope's people. They want to know if they can do their Christmas show from here.

RAYMOND

Things must be more serious than I thought. Tell me again about General Fitzhugh and the other guy.

FRED

General Fitzhugh is with the Government Rearmament Interallied Emergency Forces . . .

RAYMOND

That spells GRIEF.

FRED

That's right, sir . . . And Edward Snelling is with the United States Civilian Aid Program.

RAYMOND

That's USCAP . . .

FRED

Very good, sir. The British ambassador called. Says we made him look like a fool with his foreign office. The rest of Embassy Row isn't taking it well either.

RAYMOND

I'm sorry about that. They're all such amiable fellows.

FRED

Where's our friend Mayflower? He's had four calls this morning.

RAYMOND

I don't know if I should tell you this. He went off by himself to look into the situation up north.

FRED

Up north? He doesn't know that terrain. He'll get lost.

RAYMOND

Don't worry about Joe. He'll get through.

FRED

With our luck, he'll probably find his way back.

RAYMOND

I know you don't like Joe, but you've got to admit he's got tremendous guts.

FRED

Yes, sir. I know. His motto is: Make war, not love.

RAYMOND

That looks like a general arriving now.

FRED

I'll tell the Prince they're here.

(He goes to phone)
Go-wang da na-kori shee zu kani.

RAYMOND

Maybe they'll even call me back to Washington for consultation.

141

Counting Sheep

FRED

Ski-dung va-puts wa-shoy thug-futz Disneyland.

(Hangs up)

RAYMOND

Disneyland?

FRED

That's our code word for Washington.

(GENERAL FITZHUGH *and* EDWARD SNELLING
enter, followed by SAM, *who goes to bar*)

RAYMOND

Sorry we couldn't meet you at the airport, General, but
we've been swamped.

FRED

Welcome, Mr. Snelling. I'm Slayton, the consul. Mr.
Ambassador, Mr. Snelling.

RAYMOND

General Fitzhugh, my Number One, Fred Slayton.

GENERAL

(Opening his briefcase)

Almost got killed when we landed. There were sheep on
the runway.

RAYMOND

Sorry about that, but you know how sheep are . . . they'll
go anywhere.

142

GENERAL

First off, we're going to have to build a longer runway and put concrete over it. Or we'll never get anything in. And the sheep have to go.

SNELLING

What do you mean, the sheep have to go? Where do you want them to go?

GENERAL

I don't give a damn ... get them miles away from the airfield.

SNELLING

You can't do that—sheep raising's a major industry.

RAYMOND

How about dividing the time—one hour for the planes landing—one hour for sheep grazing ...

(*They all stare at* RAYMOND)

FRED

Gentlemen, if you put concrete on the runway, you don't have to worry about the sheep.

RAYMOND

What you boys need is a drink. Sam. What will you have?

SNELLING and **GENERAL**

(*Together*)

Vodka martini.

RAYMOND

Thank God.

SNELLING

First off, I'd like to talk about the pacification program.

GENERAL

The pacification program can come later.

SNELLING

It has to come at the beginning. We have to win the hearts and minds of these people, or the military successes will be hollow victories.

FRED

Gentlemen, I wouldn't count on military successes. Prince Gow doesn't have much of an army.

GENERAL

We'll change all that. It's just a question of the right equipment, superior intelligence, and troop morale.

SNELLING

And a good pacification program.

GENERAL

Oh, shut up.

RAYMOND

Please, gentlemen. You're both needed here, and I'm sure your organizations will complement each other.

> (GENERAL *notices* SAM *serving drinks. He falls over the map to hide it from* SAM *and mutters to* RAYMOND *to get rid of* SAM)

RAYMOND

Thanks, Sam. I'll take those.

(SAM *gives up tray and leaves*)

GENERAL

You can't be too careful with those gooks around. Now, we've been studying the situation for a week. Washington assumes the Commies control this area up here, and the royalists control this area here. General Kai must be getting his stuff through this pass. If we close the pass with intensive bombing, we cut off his supplies and he folds in a month.

RAYMOND

It makes sense to me.

FRED

There're only two things wrong with that plan, General. It would take a million tons of bombs to close that pass, and Prince Gow has no air force.

GENERAL

I'd appreciate it, young man, if you would leave the military strategy to those of us who know what we're doing. These two bridges over the Beelum River will have to be destroyed so Kai won't be able to counterattack.

SNELLING

I need those bridges for my pacification program.

FRED

Those bridges are the only way the natives can get their goods to the south.

GENERAL

Once we wipe out Kai's forces, we'll build them new bridges.

SNELLING

Will that come out of your budget or mine?

GENERAL

Destroying the bridges comes out of my budget. Rebuilding them comes out of yours.

SNELLING

Then why can't I have a say about what bridges will be destroyed?

GENERAL

Because, damn it, when it comes to destroying things, the military always has priority.

RAYMOND

Why don't we compromise and just destroy one bridge?

FRED

The decision should not be ours. Prince Gow should be the one to decide.

GENERAL

Absolutely, this is their show. The President wants it made perfectly clear that no American boys are to do any fighting. Of course, we'll have to have advisers for air and ground forces, special forces troops must be sent to teach the natives how to use our equipment, but we want them to know from the start it's their war.

(*Sound of Prince's car*)

FRED

There's the Prince now.

GENERAL

Where are the royalist troops now?

FRED

Right here in town. Most of them are guarding Prince
Gow's palace.

GENERAL

We have to get them equipped and into the field.

SNELLING

First, I want to talk to Prince Gow about land reform.

GENERAL

Let me talk to him about his army, first, goddammit.

RAYMOND

Gentlemen, gentlemen. I'm sure the Prince will be happy
to hear from both of you.

FRED

His Royal Highness, Prince Salong Gow, Exalted Ruler
of the Kingdom of Nonomura.

> (PRINCE GOW, *dressed in resplendent mar-
> shal's uniform, enters with* COLONEL NUM
> *in paratrooper's uniform and black beret.*
> EVERYONE *bows*)

RAYMOND

Your Highness, this is General Fitzhugh and Mr. Snelling
of AID.

PRINCE

Colonel Num, my minister of defense.

COLONEL

I'm extremely honored to be in the presence of the great General "Ripcord" Fitzhugh.

GENERAL

You've heard of me?

COLONEL

I was at Fort Bragg for six months' training and you were in charge of the parachute school.

GENERAL

Well, of course I remember. Well, now that I know we've got a Fort Bragg-trained officer here, I feel much more secure.

RAYMOND

Gentlemen, gentlemen, why don't you sit down and get acquainted?

(RAYMOND *and* FRED *exit into office*)

PRINCE

General, where is the equipment your country has so graciously bestowed on us?

GENERAL

I didn't bring it with me, Your Highness. I've just come to have a look-see to find out what you people need.

(*He pulls out catalogue*)

Now this is our military catalogue. Take a look through it and see if there's anything there that strikes you. Look at those bazookas, Your Highness. They're great for your kind of terrain. How many do you want?

PRINCE

Three.

GENERAL

Three? I'm afraid they don't come by threes. What about five hundred?

COLONEL

Why not? What we don't use against the Communists we can always use against the university.

GENERAL

How are you fixed for mortars?

COLONEL

We're very low on mortars. Of course, we never had any to begin with.

GENERAL

Well, let's say—one thousand mortars and ten thousand shells.

SNELLING

Your Highness, I have been sent here by the State Department in order to rebuild your economy. Now, MIT did a time-and-motion study of sheep shearing in Australia, and we've developed a brand-new battery-operated sheep-shearing clipper. Can we put you down for one thousand?

Counting Sheep

PRINCE

We have been shearing sheep from time immemorial with regular shears.

SNELLING

It takes an average of three hours and thirty-five minutes to shear a sheep by your antiquated methods. With the battery-operated clippers it would take exactly forty-three minutes.

PRINCE

But what would my people do with the time they've saved?

SNELLING

Leisure, Your Highness, leisure.

(*Going into his briefcase*)

I have a study here from UCLA on how to turn leisure time into a profit.

GENERAL

Americans make a lot of money from people doing nothing.

SNELLING

Leisure activity now accounts for eighteen cents of every dollar spent in the United States.

PRINCE

Idle people are dangerous people. I see no advantage to shearing sheep in forty-three minutes.

GENERAL

Your Highness, take a look at this tank. It's our Super
T-89 all-night, all-weather model. It's absolutely essen-
tial for clearing roadblocks.

SNELLING

Those tanks can really chew up a road. You'll need bull-
dozers to repair the roads.

PRINCE

You're going to "chew up" my roads?

SNELLING

After the tanks wreck them, my road-building equipment will put them back in better shape than they were
before.

GENERAL

Well, I'll only put you down for ten tanks to start with.
If you're unhappy with them, we'll be glad to take them
back.

SNELLING

Now, Your Highness, we would like to spray your swamps
with DDT.

PRINCE

I've read somewhere that DDT is very dangerous.

SNELLING

Well, it has been declared dangerous for the United
States, but it has not been declared dangerous for the rest
of the world. Now, on an initial investment of one million
dollars, your share would . . .

PRINCE

My share? No one said I would have to pay a share of the cost.

SNELLING

Some programs we give you an outright grant. Others, you provide the funds and we provide the know-how.

PRINCE

I am not interested in the know-how if it costs me anything.

GENERAL

The military gives you the know-how and the stuff besides; it costs you nothing. We're obligated to give it to you under the Himalayan Pact Alliance.

PRINCE

I didn't know there was a Himalayan Pact Alliance.

GENERAL

Neither did we. We had a hell of a time finding a pact that would fit your situation. By chance, the State Department discovered under the Southeast Asia Treaty Organization, we were obligated to defend Turkey, which was obligated to defend Iran, which is obligated to defend Afghanistan, which, as you know, is obligated to defend . . .

PRINCE AND COLONEL

(*Together*)

Nonomura.

GENERAL

Yes, in case of attack. You're a very fortunate man, Your Highness. Now I know you'll like this section here. We have machine guns, submachine guns, Brownings, carbines, and rocket launchers. I'll just put you down for five thousand of each of the automatic weapons.

PRINCE

But we don't have five thousand men in our army.

GENERAL

Take it while you can. The way Congress has been acting, they could cut you off at any time.

SNELLING

The way to get on the right side of Congress is to initiate a land reform program.

PRINCE

What's that?

SNELLING

What we had in mind is that you split up the large estates and divide the land among the peasants, thereby giving them a participation in the fruits of their labor.

PRINCE

Isn't that a Communist idea?

SNELLING

The Communists perverted land reform, Your Highness. Under Marxism, the land is taken away from the capitalists and given to the peasants so they will work for the state. Under our land reform system, the land is requisitioned from the landowners, who are compensated for it, and it is then given to the peasants in hopes that they will eventually become capitalists.

PRINCE

I fail to see the advantage.

SNELLING

Peasants always love to own things. They really get the old incentive when they own their own land. They work like the devil.

PRINCE

Do you have land reform in the United States?

GENERAL

Well, do we?

SNELLING

Not on the mainland, no. Now, in all due respect, Your Highness, we have found in backward countries that the landowners are one of the major factors in holding back progress. Someone with your education and progressive views could say to your landowners, "Gentlemen, we have to cut the land up."

PRINCE

That's very interesting, but I will not do it.

SNELLING

Why not?

PRINCE

I own all the land.

GENERAL

Washington should have known that, Your Highness.
Why the hell didn't Washington know that, Snelling?

SNELLING

There was no mention of it in our research, and it was
done by Princeton University.

PRINCE

General, what are these things back here?

GENERAL

That's our PX section, Your Highness.

PRINCE

There are watches and radios and refrigerators and cam-
eras and clothing and—look here—there are motorcars,
motorcars.

GENERAL

Yes, we stock everything. The American PX is the key-
stone to our military power.

PRINCE

Can I order anything available from this section of your
catalogue?

GENERAL

Naturally, Your Highness. If you're going to have a strong
defense posture, you must have a totally equipped PX.

PRINCE

Jolly good.

SNELLING

Now we shall have to discuss the question of the standard of living of the people.

PRINCE

My people have a standard of living.

SNELLING

That's correct, Your Highness, but we must raise it.

PRINCE

Why?

SNELLING

Because that's what you do with a standard of living. If your people are living in squalor.

PRINCE

My people are not living in squalor.

SNELLING

Look, all the United States is trying to do is make everyone in the world thriving members of the democratic community.

PRINCE

Democratic community?

SNELLING

Right. We are willing to aid any country, Your Highness, providing that country is willing to do its share to bring about a system of government where all the people will have a say in their own destiny.

156

PRINCE

I imagine that would include free elections and a constitution?

(RAYMOND *enters*)

SNELLING

Of course, Your Highness, that's what we're all striving for.

RAYMOND

Well, how are you gentlemen getting along?

PRINCE

He keeps talking to me about land reform. You told me there were no conditions attached to accepting American aid.

RAYMOND

There are no conditions, Your Highness. In order to get aid, you have to promise reform. Once you get the aid, then you tell us why you can't make the reforms. Countries are doing that to us all the time.

PRINCE

You want to change everything in my country.

RAYMOND

Oh, no, we don't, Your Highness.

GENERAL

Snelling just got caught up in his own rhetoric.

RAYMOND

It's all altruism, Your Highness. There's nothing in this for us.

GENERAL

We want to make Nonomuki here the showcase of the free world.

COLONEL

You're treating us like a banana republic.

PRINCE

That's it . . . a banana republic.

SNELLING

We're only trying to help you people pick yourselves up by your bootstraps.

RAYMOND

Mr. Snelling.

PRINCE

I am not interested in your civilian aid or your military aid. I will not be blackmailed into changing my government. Not for all the PX's in America.

SNELLING

What did I say wrong?

RAYMOND

Your Highness, I'm sure something can be worked out.

PRINCE

Gentlemen, I'm not interested in discussing this matter any further.

RAYMOND

Your Highness, we're only trying to help you.

PRINCE

Help? Your wife's birth control campaign? I have just issued an edict forbidding any woman in my country from taking the pill.

RAYMOND

The Pope will be happy to hear that.

COLONEL

And will you deny that your daughter is sowing seeds of discontent among our students?

PRINCE

If this continues, I will have to declare you all *persona non grata*.

GENERAL

Take a look, Your Highness. It's really beautiful merchandise.

PRINCE

No, thank you, General. I'll get my military aid elsewhere.

(*Window crash and crowd noises*)

RAYMOND

Oh, my God, my window.

(MARTHA *enters*)

MARTHA

Raymond, what's going on? There's a mob outside.

FRED

It seems to be some kind of a demonstration.

159

PRINCE
We don't have demonstrations.

COLONEL
We don't allow demonstrations.

RAYMOND
They're coming this way.

GENERAL
They're carrying signs.

SNELLING
They look like students.

RAYMOND
They are students.

(COLONEL *laughs*)

COLONEL
This is an anti-American demonstration.

MARTHA
Oh, my God, Raymond . . .

RAYMOND
I might have known. She's right in the front.

(GOW *and the* COLONEL *laugh.* CROWD *chanting changes. They stop laughing and rush toward the center doors*)

GENERAL
What is it? What's going on out there?

SNELLING

Now what's the matter?

COLONEL

They're shouting, "Down with the Prince." That's what's the matter. This is treason!

(*The next five speeches are all said together*)

RAYMOND

No, it isn't.

COLONEL

This is intolerable.

GENERAL

Colonel, Your Highness.

MARTHA

I'm sure Holly has an explanation.

RAYMOND

I'll have a heart-to-heart talk with her.

PRINCE

Mr. Ambassador, I officially declare you *persona non grata.*

(EVERYONE *ad libs till* PRINCE *and* COLONEL *exit*)

RAYMOND

(*Turns downstage directly to audience*)

Oh, God, the shame of it all! I'm being kicked out of a country no one's even heard of!

CURTAIN FALLS ON ACT I

Act I

Scene *1*   *The next morning. When curtain rises, w*
             see RAYMOND, GENERAL, *and* SNELLIN
             with coats off, pacing. FRED *is walking i*
             and out of office.

RAYMOND
I'm the first ambassador under the Nixon administratio
to be declared *persona non grata.*

GENERAL
I think we're all being unduly pessimistic. The Princ
has got to come back.

RAYMOND
He's a proud man.

SNELLING
He struck me as a stubborn man.

GENERAL
He's not a stubborn man. He's a businessman.

SNELLING
He happens to be very touchy.

GENERAL
He's not touchy. He's not touchy at all. He's shrewd. He
shrewd as they come.

162

RAYMOND

Typical Oriental ... is what he is.

FRED

Gentlemen, I hate to interrupt, but we have to let Washington know very soon.

GENERAL

Know what?

FRED

That we've all been declared *persona non grata.*

(ALL *talk at once*)

GENERAL

Oh, no!

RAYMOND

No ... no.

SNELLING

Not yet.

RAYMOND

We need more time.

FRED

But, sir, Washington has to know.

RAYMOND

Why does Washington have to know?

FRED

If they declare our ambassador *persona non grata,* we have to declare the Prince's ambassador *persona non grata* at the same time—or we'll lose face.

163

RAYMOND

Oh, is that the way it works?

FRED

Yes, sir.

GENERAL

Good God, what a mess. Wait till I go back to the Pentagon and tell them we couldn't get rid of the stuff. We've got to get rid of the stuff, or we won't have any place to put the new stuff.

SNELLING

I don't know how we can have an aid program if people won't take our aid.

RAYMOND

All I know is I got along great with the Prince until you guys arrived.

(*Looks at* FRED)

What the devil are you doing?

FRED

I'm burning all our classified documents.

RAYMOND

I didn't know we had any.

(*Phone rings*)

FRED

Wa-shu fug—walli er shoots scaz-moose.

SNELLING

What's that all about?

GENERAL

Who was it?

FRED

The Prince is on his way over.

(ALL *rush to get ready for Prince*)

FRED

Sir, I've burned all our classified documents.

RAYMOND

Never mind. We'll get more.

SNELLING

You see, you see, he wants his swamps sprayed.

GENERAL

He doesn't want his swamps sprayed. This is what he wants. My PX stuff. If you so much as mention land reform . . .

RAYMOND

Gentlemen, let's not be overeager. We're dealing with the inscrutable East. It is all soft sell out here, all soft sell.

(FRED *goes to door. A Nonomuran* SOLDIER *comes in.* EVERYONE *bows, expecting the Prince; instead it is* HOLLY. SOLDIER *exits*)

RAYMOND

Holly, where the hell have you been?

HOLLY

You and your stupid diplomatic immunity. They threw me out of jail.

FRED

You were in jail?

HOLLY

You should have seen it. No water, no food, twenty kids in one little cell.

RAYMOND

It's everything she's ever dreamed of. Martha! This is the end ... the bitter end ... Martha. Madame Trotsky has returned.

(MARTHA *enters*)

MARTHA

Holly, are you all right?

RAYMOND

She's furious because she didn't get twenty years.

MARTHA

Do you realize that you have destroyed your father's career as an ambassador?

FRED

If you'd only just stuck to your anti-American demonstrations ... the Prince didn't mind that.

GENERAL

There's a lot more at stake here, young lady, than your sophomoric demonstrations.

MARTHA

Perhaps if she personally apologized to the Prince ...

HOLLY

Why should I apologize? I'm not sorry for anything. I'm starved. As soon as I get something to eat, I'm going to picket the palace.

FRED

You can't leave the embassy, Holly.

HOLLY

Why not?

RAYMOND

Because I said so.

FRED

You're still an American citizen, so this embassy is responsible for you. You'd better let me hold onto your passport.

HOLLY

Not on your life.

MARTHA

Let him hold onto your passport.

FRED

I'll return it to you at the airport.

HOLLY

You know what you are, Mr. Slayton? You're a bureaucrat!

MARTHA

Holly! Apologize this instant!

(*Sound—Prince's horn*)

167

SNELLING
It's the Prince.

HOLLY
I'm not apologizing to anyone. I may be *persona non grata,* but I've just begun to fight!

(HOLLY *exits*)

RAYMOND
Martha, lock her up before she screws us up again.

GENERAL
Now, remember, Snelling, let him shear his sheep any goddamn way he wants.

FRED
His Royal Highness, Prince Salong Gow, Exalted Ruler of the Kingdom of Nonomura.

COLONEL
Your passports please, gentlemen.

GENERAL
Passports?

COLONEL
You will remain in the embassy until suitable transportation is available to take you home.

SNELLING
Now what did we do?

PRINCE
Do you realize that thanks to all of you, I have been called an American puppet?

RAYMOND
Who would call you that?

PRINCE
The Chinese, the Burmese, the Nepalese, the Indians—
the whole world.

GENERAL
That's ridiculous.

RAYMOND
You're overreacting.

PRINCE
In twelve hundred years, no one has ever called anyone
in my family a puppet.

RAYMOND
Your Highness, there are worse things to be called than
a puppet.

SNELLING
We've had some very fine American puppets in our
history.

PRINCE
I have come here to order Washington to announce that
I have not accepted one cent of American aid and I have
no intention of doing so and I demand an official apology
from your government.

COLONEL
And if Washington does not respond to His Highness'
demands, the consequences will be grave.

(*As* PRINCE *and* NUM *start to exit,* JOE *staggers in past them*)

RAYMOND

Joe!

GENERAL

Joe Mayflower!

JOE

Water, water, bottled water, please.

(*Collapses on pillow, recovers, and says*)

My God, what a trip.

RAYMOND

Joe, are you all right?

JOE

My jeep broke down. I traveled the last ten miles by buffalo. Ripcord, for crying out loud ...

GENERAL

You old son of a gun.

JOE

Ah, Your Highness, glad you're here. Who's this?

GENERAL

Colonel Num, minister of defense.

JOE

Glad you're here, Colonel. I was up in the highlands. I don't like the look of things.

GENERAL

What's up, Joe?

JOE

The country's teeming with activity . . . things are boiling up there . . . wherever I went you could feel it.

RAYMOND

What did you see? Who did you talk to?

JOE

That's just it. I didn't see a soul. I didn't talk to anyone.

RAYMOND

So?

JOE

So where is everyone? Why are they hiding from me? Tell me that.

PRINCE

I don't know.

JOE

You bet you don't know! Curious, isn't it?

FRED

Where did you go?

JOE

How do I know where I went? I'm a stranger here.

FRED

You must have been in an isolated area. Where there are no people.

JOE

Nonsense. I'll tell you where they are. Training somewhere. Probably with Chinese hardware.

COLONEL

Chinese hardware?

JOE

Who else would equip them? We didn't. Your Highness, I'm sure the Chinese are up at Kai's headquarters.

PRINCE

The Chinese?

JOE

This thing is going even better than we hoped it would. We have a wonderful major threat.

PRINCE

I didn't want a threat that badly.

GENERAL

You've got to face up to it, Your Highness. Kai is probably mounting an offensive right now.

PRINCE

I can't believe Kai would launch an offensive. He's far too lazy.

SNELLING

I'm certainly glad to see you, Mr. Mayflower.

JOE

Who's this?

FRED

Snelling, AID.

SNELLING

It's good that you came when you did, because we have just been declared *persona non grata*.

JOE

Persona non grata? That's out of the question, Your Highness. We have to start cracking. Once Kai's equipped, he'll probably move south.

PRINCE

(*To* COLONEL)

What troops do we have in the north?

COLONEL

Major Tang, Your Highness.

PRINCE

Oh, him.

COLONEL

You sent him up there to get him away from your sister.

JOE

Your Highness, I can smell a Communist offensive a hundred miles away. There's only one thing that can save you now.

GENERAL

Strength!

JOE

Precisely.

Counting Sheep

RAYMOND

The best way to avoid war is to prepare for it.

SNELLING

A bird in the hand is worth two in the bush.

PRINCE

But if I accept your aid . . . a bird in the hand? If I accept your aid, I will lose face.

JOE

And if you don't, you'll lose your country.

COLONEL

I don't like it, Your Highness.

PRINCE

Nobody likes it, Colonel. What part don't you like?

COLONEL

I don't like the Chinese being in the north.

PRINCE

For twelve hundred years, we've kept the Chinese out.

GENERAL

And we'll keep them out again.

PRINCE

You think this is a good idea, Colonel?

COLONEL

I don't see that we have any choice.

JOE

You're not marrying us, Your Highness.

174

SNELLING

We'll just be sleeping together.

JOE

Your Highness, I am going to write a column in my four
hundred newspapers telling the world that you are holding off the Chinese hordes single-handedly.

RAYMOND

And when he does, the name of Gow will become a house-
hold word.

PRINCE

Thank you, but you've done enough for me already.

JOE

The only important thing is for you to keep your throne.

PRINCE

I wish I had my astrologer here.

(*Capitulates*)

General, how many Americans do you think it will take to
train the Nonomuran Army?

GENERAL

Let's see. The military aid staff, support troops for the
military aid staff, drivers, specialists, support troops for
the specialists, rest and recreation, armed forces radio,
support troops for the armed forces radio.

RAYMOND

Don't forget the Officers' Club.

GENERAL

Right. Then we have an NCO Club and an enlisted men's club. The Navy will want in.

PRINCE

But we're a landlocked country.

GENERAL

Gotta let the Navy in or they'll raise Cain. We'll let them do river patrols and run the laundry. All told, I think that we can do it with twenty-five hundred—to start with.

SNELLING

And I've only got three men assigned to me for the entire pacification program.

PRINCE

General, I'll expect you to attend my cabinet meeting this afternoon.

GENERAL

I'll be honored.

COLONEL

I hope you'll review our parachute brigade, General.

GENERAL

Be delighted. How many jumps have they made?

COLONEL

None.

GENERAL

None?

176

COLONEL

We have no parachutes.

PRINCE

We have no planes.

GENERAL

Planes, planes—how could I have forgotten planes? Don't worry about it, Your Highness, you'll get planes. Take this along with you. If you see anything that grabs you, give me a ring.

PRINCE

Thank you, General. I've been giving it some thought . . . I want the PX right next to the palace.

(PRINCE *is about to exit as* HOLLY *enters carrying a list. She accosts the* PRINCE)

HOLLY

Your Highness, as the daughter of His Excellency, the Ambassador of the United States of America, I have here a list of nonnegotiable demands: one, immediate release and amnesty for all university students; two, equal rights for all women of Nonomura; three, the abolishment of the concubine system.

PRINCE

(*Stunned*)

Mr. Ambassador . . .

RAYMOND

She's leaving! She's leaving! She's leaving on the next plane.

(*He rushes her out*)

PRINCE

Equal rights for women. We don't have equal rights for men.

(NUM *and* PRINCE *exit*)

GENERAL

I have to hand it to you, Joe. You saved my butt with Washington.

(RAYMOND *reenters*)

JOE

You're losing your touch, Ripcord, if you let the prince of a fourth-rate power push you around.

GENERAL

Now wait a minute, let's not forget these people don't have to take our equipment just because it is offered to them.

FRED

In my opinion they were doing fine without it.

JOE

Oh, stop that talk, young man. Our job is to keep all neutral countries in the Western camp. There is no better way to do it than by training and equipping their military people.

SNELLING

But it can't be done without raising the standard of living. The natives must be made to see that the road to capitalism is the best. We can only do this by increasing the gross national product.

178

GENERAL

Ah, shut up.

JOE

But first we have got to win the war.

FRED

What war? I still say we have absolutely no evidence that Kai wants to come south.

JOE

You seem to have forgotten, Slayton, that we only recognize the government of Prince Gow. We don't do business with bandits.

FRED

But you don't need twenty-five hundred advisers and free military equipment and fighter bombers not to do business with them.

JOE

I'll leave it to Raymond. He's the ambassador. Well, Raymond?

RAYMOND

Well, ah—I naturally don't want to do anything to upset the balance of power out here. At the same time, we can't have anyone spitting on the American flag. It's true that things have been quiet, but it could be a lull before the storm. There's a lot to be said for neutrality, because once you're committed, it is very hard to get out of that commitment, but if we have to choose between strength and weakness, and I'm not saying that we do, all I say is— let's not forget the price of vigilance.

FRED

Sir, what is your decision?

RAYMOND

That's my decision.

GENERAL

That's right, Mr. Ambassador. You send in your report and I'll send in mine and we'll get action immediately.

JOE

"Done and Done." I'm going upstairs and have my first bath in a week. God, I feel good. There's nothing like a danger from the north to get the old juices flowing.

RAYMOND

Thank goodness you arrived when you did, Joe. Well, I'd say this was a very successful meeting. Oh, there's one problem I'd hoped you'd help me out with, General.

GENERAL

What's that?

RAYMOND

Could you get me a new plate glass for my dining room window?

GENERAL

I'm not too sure that we have plate glass. The military doesn't have much use for it. Snelling here could probably get it for you faster.

SNELLING

We have plate glass.

180

RAYMOND

You do?

SNELLING

Oh, yes. It's a big item for American embassies nowadays.

(SNELLING *exits with the* GENERAL)

RAYMOND

I'm sorry, Fred, but these are lonely decisions and only an ambassador can make them.

FRED

Yes, sir.

(FRED *exits;* SAM *enters*)

RAYMOND

Sam, you'll never know how close we came to being booted out of here. But, I want you to know one thing: If we had to go, we would have taken you with us. You'd love Chevy Chase. Raymond Wilkins respects one thing more than anything else in the world, and that's loyalty. You don't understand a goddamn thing I'm saying.

(RAYMOND *exits.* SAM *goes to balcony, gives three owl calls, and there are three answering calls. Then, he blows parachute from duster.*
Blackout)

Act II

Scene 2   *Some time later.* Two Nonomurans *carrying large picture window of glass cross into dining room.* Raymond *stops centerstage as* Martha *enters.*

RAYMOND
We'd have never gotten that piece of glass if Washington hadn't declared us a crisis area.

MARTHA
I suppose that since there's a crisis, we weren't wrong to send Holly home. But she hasn't written. She promised to write us as soon as she got home. I wonder why she hasn't written.

RAYMOND
Probably too busy arranging to burn down Radcliffe.

(Tank noises from street)

What's that?

MARTHA
I don't know.

RAYMOND
They're tanks coming down the street.

GENERAL

Have I gotta surprise! Have I gotta surprise! The stuff's
arrived.

(JOE *comes rushing in*)

JOE

What's up, Rip?

GENERAL

Feast your eyes on that, Joe.

JOE

How'd it get here so fast?

GENERAL

They were on their way to India, but India refused them
because we had just given planes to Pakistan. So they
were sent to Malaysia, who turned them down when they
heard we were sending jeeps to Indonesia. Then they
were rerouted to Ceylon, but the British got wind of it
and griped because they have an arms contract with the
Ceylonese.

JOE

Is it OK with the Pentagon?

GENERAL

Pentagon? They don't even know where the stuff is . . .

(*Sound of screeching tanks*)

SNELLING

Who's that in the first tank? It almost hit the Buddhist
temple.

183

Counting Sheep

GENERAL

Hey, it's Colonel Num. Like a kid with a new toy!

MARTHA

What are those big things?

GENERAL

Weapon carriers . . .

MARTHA

They're knocking down those beautiful old trees.

SNELLING

Why are they driving the stuff when they don't know how?

GENERAL

Oh, they always knock down a few trees, a couple of shops, and an occasional shrine until they get the hang of it.

JOE

Those amphibious armored cars . . . beautiful.

GENERAL

Great for rice paddies.

SNELLING

You promised you wouldn't go into the rice paddies.

GENERAL

If Charlie's in the rice paddies, we're going into the rice paddies.

MARTHA

Look at those trucks . . . refrigerators . . .

184

RAYMOND

TV sets . . . clothes . . .

GENERAL

That's the PX stuff coming in . . .

JOE

What about aircraft, Rip?

GENERAL

They'll be coming. They have to give us the aircraft to
protect the stuff.

MARTHA

Look at the people on the street. They seem terribly ex-
cited about the whole thing.

GENERAL

Happens every time. You send a few tanks down the
main street of a capital . . . cheers up the whole country.

RAYMOND

Those people down there, they're setting up stands.

SNELLING

My God, no.

RAYMOND

What?

SNELLING

They're starting a black market.

GENERAL

Well, what do you know!

RAYMOND

Those trucks are just unloading and they're at it already.

GENERAL

You've got to admire their spirit.

SNELLING

That stuff was supposed to be for my pacification program.

GENERAL

Don't worry, Snelling. We're going to pacify this place like it's never been pacified before.

FRED

(Entering from office)

Mr. Mayflower, this cable just came for you.

RAYMOND

Fred, you see it? All that material coming in.

FRED

I saw it. General, did the State Department know this material was coming here?

GENERAL

Of course they knew. We always inform State after we've done something.

RAYMOND

No one's going to get hurt, Fred.

SNELLING

All we want for them is to have the good things in life.

GENERAL

And you can't have the good things in life unless you protect the things from some son of a bitch who's going to take them away from you.

JOE

(*Looking up from cable*)

Raymond, what the hell have you done?

RAYMOND

What do you mean?

JOE

How do you explain this cable?

(*Reads*)

Ambassador Wilkins just sent report to State, advising that crisis in Nonomura subsiding and Communist threat nonexistent. Your columns do not gel with this. If State releases Wilkins' report, we'll have jam on our faces.

RAYMOND

I sent no such report.

GENERAL

Crisis subsiding? All that stuff out there . . . That's crisis stuff.

JOE

You made me into a horse's ass.

187

Counting Sheep

MARTHA

Raymond didn't make you into a horse's ass. Raymond would never make you into a horse's ass. I don't know anyone who would make you into a horse's ass, Joe.

FRED

I made you into a horse's ass.

JOE

What?

FRED

I sent that report.

RAYMOND

You sent a report under my name?

FRED

Sir, I've always done that.

RAYMOND

But you said the crisis was subsiding.

FRED

Yes, sir.

JOE

Well, Raymond. What do you think of your protégé now?

RAYMOND

You must have an explanation.

FRED

The only explanation I have, sir, is that I was trying to stop this charade from getting out of hand.

188

RAYMOND
Fred, Nonomura will be a better place for what we're doing here today.

MARTHA
The United States wouldn't be where it is today if it didn't know what was good for the rest of the world.

FRED
Perhaps. But I'm resigning.

MARTHA
Fred, you wouldn't leave Raymond in the lurch.

RAYMOND
Fred, you can't leave now. This embassy needs you.

FRED
Mr. Ambassador, nobody needs us. We are just errand boys for the Pentagon and some faceless guys in the bowels of the White House . . . And a hysterical columnist who writes for four hundred newspapers. It's no good, sir. You're just going to have to find yourself another bureaucrat.

(FRED *exits*)

JOE
I have always said . . . never trust a man who speaks the language of the country where he's stationed.

GENERAL
I know those kids, they all want to remake the world. They're presumptuous, self-righteous, and arrogant, just like my own kid.

JOE

I knew he was untrustworthy. I'm pretty sure he's been tampering with my papers.

MARTHA

Oh, no, Joe, that's impossible.

RAYMOND

Fred would never do that. I'd stake my life on it.

JOE

(*Small tantrum*)

Stake your life on it? Damn it, haven't you learned yet that nobody can trust anybody? I don't trust anybody. I've never trusted anybody, and I'm proud to say that no one has ever trusted me . . . I tell you that somebody's been tampering with my papers and I can prove it. I was suspicious two days ago, so I planted some dental floss on my papers. For two days' running, the dental floss has been disturbed. It's a trick I learned from Allen Dulles.

RAYMOND

By God, he's right. This dental floss is disturbed. But no one could have gotten into the embassy. Sam's on watch all the time.

GENERAL

I was going to ask you about him. Have you had a security check on him?

RAYMOND

His references seemed to be in order. We got him from the British embassy.

MARTHA

Sam couldn't be a spy. He's so neat and serves so well.

GENERAL

Let's have a little talk with him anyway.

RAYMOND

(*Starting out dining-room door*)

Sam!

GENERAL

During World War II, the British ambassador had a German spy working as a butler and this spy stole the plans for D Day.

SNELLING

That was James Mason.

JOE

James Mason played the role of the spy. The man's name was Cicero.

RAYMOND

(*From offstage*)

Sam . . . Sam . . .

GENERAL

Who's in charge of security around here:

RAYMOND

(*From offstage*)

Sam!

MARTHA

I really don't know. It could have been Fred.

JOE

Of course. Doves never worry about security.

MARTHA

I hope Sam's not a spy. I don't think I could train another butler again.

RAYMOND

(*Reenters*)

He's gone . . . disappeared. No trace of him.

JOE

When's the last time anyone saw him?

MARTHA

Last night at dinner.

GENERAL

This is serious. We'd better notify Washington at once.

SNELLING

I hope he didn't see my reports. They were done by the Political Science Department of the University of Wisconsin.

GENERAL

He saw my map.

SNELLING

That map appeared in *Time* magazine last week.

RAYMOND
Should we notify the Prince?

GENERAL
We'd better not. He'll lose confidence in us if he finds out how lousy our security is.

(*Two explosions*)

MARTHA
What religious holiday are they celebrating now?

RAYMOND
I have no idea.

(*Sounds of gunfire*)

JOE
They don't sound like fireworks to me.

GENERAL
By God, that's gunfire. Hit the floor, everybody.

(THEY ALL *drop to the floor*)

JOE
Could Kai have gotten here already?

GENERAL
Who else could it be?

JOE
I'm going to crawl out and have a look. I'm not going to be intimidated by a handful of Kai's bandits.

RAYMOND
No. No, I'll go, Joe. I have diplomatic immunity.

(*Loud explosion and gunfire*)

GENERAL

I'll handle this. Everybody stay back.

(GENERAL *crawls.* MARTHA *is in his path.*
He crawls over her)

Sorry, Mrs. Wilkins.

MARTHA

That's all right, General.

GENERAL

(*He gets to balcony*)

Boy, oh, boy, oh, boy, oh, boy.

SNELLING

What do you see, General?

GENERAL

I don't see anything . . . I don't know what's happening.

(*Single shot . . . window crashes*)

RAYMOND

Oh, God, my window.

(*Phone rings*)

Oh, God, the phone.

(*Goes to phone, steps over* SNELLING, *who*
is in his path)

Hello . . .

(*Aside*)

God, it's the Secretary of State . . . Yes, Mr. Secretary. The situation here?

(Aside, in panic)

He wants to know about the situation here . . .

JOE

Stall him. Tell him anything.

RAYMOND

Call me back. I'm in the shower!

(Hangs up)

My God, what did I do! I hung up on the Secretary of State. What did I do!

(PRINCE GOW breaks into room, disheveled and tattered)

MARTHA

Your Highness . . .

JOE

What's going on out there?

GENERAL

What's all the shooting about?

PRINCE

What's all the shooting about? Colonel Num just took over my palace.

RAYMOND

Colonel Num?

PRINCE

My own minister of defense, the man you trained at Fort Bragg. He took all your tanks and surrounded my palace and took it over.

GENERAL

Good God.

SNELLING

Holy smokes.

RAYMOND

It's obvious he exceeded his authority.

PRINCE

I hold you all responsible.

JOE

Now look here, Your Highness . . .

PRINCE

You started this whole thing, with your threats and your armaments, and I want you to get me my throne back.

RAYMOND

And you should have it, Your Highness.

GENERAL

That's right, we never gave that stuff to Colonel Num.

JOE

You know, I never trusted Colonel Num.

GENERAL

Why not?

JOE

Why should I?

RAYMOND

We will never recognize Colonel Num.

PRINCE

That's good.

GENERAL

And we'll see to it that he returns all those tanks to you.

PRINCE

That's nice.

SNELLING

And if there's been any damage to the palace, we'll repair it.

PRINCE

All right.

RAYMOND

Is that satisfactory?

PRINCE

Yes, that's satisfactory. Very satisfactory. And after I get my throne back, I want all of you to get out of my country.

RAYMOND

Get out of the country?

PRINCE

Of course.

JOE

Do you realize whom you are telling to get out of your country? You are talking to the representative of the greatest sovereign nation on earth, the bastion of the free world. When you are talking to this man, you are talking to the President of the United States.

RAYMOND

The man who gave you that very valuable photograph of himself and his wife.

PRINCE

Oh. I almost forgot that, but I'd still like you to leave . . .

> (*Suddenly two bayonets are shoved through the door.* TWO NONOMURAN SOLDIERS *enter.* EVERYONE *backs away.* COLONEL NUM *strides in cockily, carrying a decree in his hand*)

COLONEL

(Unrolls declaration)

On behalf of the First Nonomuran Provisional Republic, I hereby declare a state of martial law. Anyone interfering with the ruling military junta, which shall remain in power until free elections are held at some future unspecified time, will be summarily executed and all properties confiscated. Signed by the executive order of Premier Num.

GENERAL

Premier Num?

COLONEL

I have a warrant for the arrest of Prince Gow.

RAYMOND

May I remind you, sir, that you are now on American soil.

PRINCE

Colonel, your troops will be pardoned, but as for you . . . you know the punishment for treason.

COLONEL

I am the premier.

PRINCE

But I am the prince. Tell him, Mr. Ambassador. Tell him what you just told me.

RAYMOND

Tell him what?

PRINCE

About getting my throne back. And all the other things. Tell him.

GENERAL

Colonel, that military equipment was given for defense purposes, not *coup d'état* purposes.

JOE

Good try, Colonel. But the Prince is the one we deal with.

RAYMOND

Come on, Colonel, give him back his throne.

COLONEL

Gentlemen, Prince Gow is a neutralist.

Counting Sheep

Joe *and* General

(*Together*)

A neutralist!

COLONEL

You heard me.

JOE

Is that true, Your Highness?

PRINCE

I had no intention of going to war, if that's what you mean. I told you that from the beginning.

GENERAL

But you took our catalogue.

COLONEL

The Prince has no interest in the modern world. We are tired of having parachute troops who have no parachutes, a palace guard dressed for an operetta. We will achieve discipline, efficiency, and order, and we will instill pride and a new spirit of nationalism in the people of Nonomura.

PRINCE

Horse shit!

GENERAL

Still, I think we should examine the situation carefully.

PRINCE

But, General, you promised.

The Play

GENERAL

Your Highness, it's true Colonel Num didn't do this as
neatly as I would have liked, but he was trained at Fort
Bragg.

PRINCE

Mr. Ambassador . . .

RAYMOND

This is a completely new development and I will have
to clear it with Washington . . .

PRINCE

Mr. Mayflower . . . I appeal to you . . .

JOE

Your Highness, the United States never interferes with a
military coup provided it's not from the left.

PRINCE

Mr. Snelling . . .

SNELLING

Ah, ahhh.

PRINCE

Oh, forget it.

COLONEL

Gentlemen, may I remind you that I control those tanks
out there? Shall we go, Your Highness?

SNELLING

What are you going to do with him?

201

COLONEL

Shoot him.

RAYMOND

My God, is that necessary?

COLONEL

I have to shoot him to prove I'm in charge.

JOE

Public opinion could go against you. I've made the Prince into a folk hero.

GENERAL

Don't complicate your coup, Colonel.

COLONEL

I'm sorry. But he must be shot.

RAYMOND

(Angrily)

Well, you're damn well not going to shoot him as long as I'm ambassador and he's in the American embassy. I'm giving him asylum.

COLONEL

But no one will believe I'm in charge.

JOE

Shooting is so old-fashioned. Make him an ambassador.

COLONEL

Very well. I can do nothing while the Prince remains in

202

your embassy, Mr. Ambassador. But if he so much as puts his foot outside the door, he will be shot.

(*He starts to exit*)

Let me remind you all that this country is under martial law. Mr. Mayflower, if you wish a statement for the press, you may say that my government is pro-Western, and I look to the United States for guidance in this grave hour of crisis. And I will be happy to meet with your President on Midway Island.

(*He exits*)

GENERAL
Boy, he learned too much at Fort Bragg.

RAYMOND
Sorry about this, Your Highness.

JOE
One way or another, we'll get you out of here.

PRINCE
What do you mean . . . one way or another?

GENERAL
Don't worry. We'll have you out of the country in no time.

PRINCE
But what will I do? Where will I go?

RAYMOND
How about setting up a government in exile on the Riviera?

(*Two shots and* COLONEL NUM *reenters*)

COLONEL

Someone's taken over my palace.

GENERAL

Christ! This is worse than Panama.

RAYMOND

Who took over your palace?

COLONEL

I don't know. My own bodyguards tried to shoot me.

GENERAL

We've got to find out who took over . . .

JOE

I was afraid something like this would happen.

GENERAL

Snelling, get on the Telex and call Synsap on the scrambler and ask if they know what's happened.

SNELLING

Telex, Synsap, scrambler, right.

(*He exits to office*)

COLONEL

Mr. Ambassador, I must formally request asylum.

RAYMOND

Asylum? You got us in a hell of a mess. Now, get out of my embassy.

204

The Play

GENERAL

Doesn't anybody around here know what the hell has happened?

COLONEL

I can't leave the embassy ... they will shoot me.

RAYMOND

You mean I have to give you asylum, too?

JOE

The students. Couldn't the students have grabbed the palace?

MARTHA

Raymond, we have only one bed in the guest room.

RAYMOND

If the students took it over, they'd give it back. Wouldn't they?

PRINCE

I was given asylum first. I get the guest room.

COLONEL

I was premier last. I should get the room.

PRINCE

Only two minutes ago he wanted to shoot me.

COLONEL

If I had, I would have gotten the room.

(SNELLING *enters*)

SNELLING

I got General Foley at Synsap.

JOE

Well?

SNELLING

He doesn't know a thing.

COLONEL

I get the room.

RAYMOND

Will you both keep quiet?

> (*Loud knock.* SOLDIER *enters with letter.*
> RAYMOND *takes letter and starts reading*)

The premier of the Second Provisional Government . . .

COLONEL

Second Provisional Government?

RAYMOND

Sends his respects and wishes to announce the country is under martial law. I order that no one leave the embassy until my personal representative arrives to discuss matters of mutual interest to our respective countries.

JOE

Who's it signed by?

RAYMOND

General Hung Kai.

> (*Next three lines are said together*)

GENERAL

My God.

JOE

I'll be damned.

SNELLING

It's worse than we thought.

JOE

What a blow to the free world!

GENERAL

Free world, my ass. What about the Pentagon? All our stuff's in Communist hands. My God, the planes. We've got to stop the planes from coming. Snelling, get on the Telex pronto and have Synsap call me on the phone immediately.

SNELLING

Telex pronto, Synsap. Roger.

(*He exits into office*)

RAYMOND

What about the Himalayan Pact Alliance?

GENERAL

No, it doesn't apply.

COLONEL

Don't you have to come to our defense?

GENERAL

Not unless someone attacks Afghanistan after they attack Turkey after they attack Iran.

JOE
Well, that can be arranged.

PRINCE
It was so nice when we were a backward country.

> (*Phone rings as* SNELLING *reenters.* GEN-
> ERAL *rushes to phone*)

GENERAL
Synsap? . . . General Fitzhugh . . . Little emergency here.
Put Plan B into operation at once. That's right—Plan B.

(Hangs up)

At least that will stop the planes from being delivered.

RAYMOND
This will look great in the New York *Times* . . . Nixon
ambassador loses country twice in one day.

JOE
Damn it, Raymond, you're always thinking of yourself.
How do I explain this disastrous turn of events?

RAYMOND
Well, you explain it by saying you're a horse's ass. Like
Fred said you were.

JOE
Raymond, don't force me to write a column telling everyone what a botch you've made of things here.

MARTHA
Raymond did not make a botch of things.

JOE

Well, if he isn't responsible, who is?

SNELLING

He wouldn't let me put my pacification program into effect. Remember I told you we had to win the natives over before the stuff arrived.

GENERAL

Don't try to weasel out of it, Snelling. You've got a lot of explaining to do in Washington as to why the natives went over to the other side.

SNELLING

(*Pointing to* COLONEL)

It's his fault. He had a weak government.

COLONEL

I didn't have a chance to form a government, so how could it be weak?

SNELLING

(*Points to* PRINCE)

If the Prince had allowed me to put in land reform.

JOE

How could you people do this to me? How could you do it! I guaranteed my readers that you would support the West, Your Highness, and I got you the equipment to defend yourself, and you let it fall into his hands. And the colonel let it fall into Kai's hands. And Ripcord, I assured my readers you had the situation under control. And you, Raymond, I was counting on your diplomatic know-how, and what did you know? Nothing. And you.

(*Turns to* SNELLING *and dismisses him*)

I'm disappointed in all of you. I'm very hurt. Hurt and disappointed. You put jam on my face.

PRINCE

Will you ever forgive us?

(HOLLY *suddenly enters. She's dressed in army guerrilla outfit with two bandoliers crisscrossed over her shoulders and a webbing gun belt with gun in holster*)

RAYMOND

Who the hell are you?

MARTHA

My God, it's Holly!

RAYMOND

Holly, who?

HOLLY

It's me, Daddy.

RAYMOND

Holly! What the hell are you doing here?

HOLLY

I never left Nonomura. I was up in the hills with General Hung Kai.

MARTHA

Up in the hills? You're supposed to be at Radcliffe. You'll
fail all your courses.

HOLLY

I was fighting for the freedom of Nonomura against the
tyranny and oppression of the monarch ... I'm sorry,
Your Highness.

PRINCE

That's all right. I'm getting used to it.

HOLLY

Daddy, General Hung Kai is the leader of the freedom-
loving people of Nonomura, and we must recognize him.

(ALL *ad lib against this*)

Daddy, please. I'll never ask you for anything again.

MARTHA

Raymond, what's happening to us?

RAYMOND

I'll tell you what's happening, Martha. We've become the
parents of a teen-aged guerrilla.

(*Sound of* PRINCE's *car*)

PRINCE

That's my Rolls-Royce.

GENERAL

It must be Hung Kai's representative.

RAYMOND

Good God.

GENERAL

What?

RAYMOND

It's my butler, Sam.

SNELLING

The guy with the dental floss?

JOE

It's obvious he wasn't small potatoes in this operation. I told you he was a Communist spy.

RAYMOND

Do you realize I have to negotiate with my own butler?

(Two SOLDIERS *enter, followed by* SAM)

SAM

Mr. Ambassador, I came to apprise you of the situation as it has developed in this country.

RAYMOND

You speak English.

SAM

I'm an American. I work for the CIA.

RAYMOND

And to think I trusted you.

SAM

It's not that bad—the CIA is on the American side. Now, first off, I'd like to advise you . . .

GENERAL

But you're here representing General Hung Kai.

SAM

That's what I'm here to tell you. He works for the CIA, too.

JOE

How can he? He's a Communist.

SAM

He was never a Communist. He was our eyes and ears in the north.

GENERAL

The usual dirty, sneaky, little CIA operation.

HOLLY

But that means General Kai isn't for the student revolution.

SAM

I would hardly say so.

HOLLY

I've been betrayed by the Establishment again.

(*Starts crying, rushes into mother's arms*)

MARTHA

We must learn we can't have everything we want in life.

(*Exits with* HOLLY)

RAYMOND

Well, let this be a lesson to her. The only one you can trust in this world is your mummy and your daddy.

213

GENERAL

Now let's hear about this dirty, sneaky, little CIA operation.

SAM

It was a perfect little operation. We put out the word that Kai was a Communist to convince the Chinese that he was on their side. It was done with such finesse that even Mayflower took the bait.

JOE

I took nobody's bait.

RAYMOND

I don't understand any of it.

SAM

The only thing we hadn't figured on was that Mayflower would be taken seriously by the powers that be in Washington.

JOE

The CIA will learn to its sorrow that Joseph Mayflower is always taken seriously. My facts may sometimes be wrong, but my judgment is always right.

GENERAL

It's going to take the Pentagon a long time to get over this one. Screwed by the CIA.

SAM

Well, you win one, you lose one.

JOE

Now, gentlemen, Pentagon, CIA, State Department—what we've done here is good for the West. And I'm proud to have played a small part in getting this operation off the ground.

RAYMOND

But, Joe, you misled the whole world by calling Hung Kai a Communist.

JOE

Well, a man can change his mind.

RAYMOND

You've changed your mind?

JOE

No, damn it. Hung Kai changed his. Last week he was a Communist. This week he's a defector. Why can't you see that? Tomorrow the whole world will read about the greatest Communist defector of all times. Gentlemen, my judgment may occasionally be wrong, but my facts are always right.

(*Phone rings*)

RAYMOND

Hello . . . Yes . . . oh.

(*Aside*)

My God, the Secretary's calling from a Cabinet meeting at the White House. Yes, sir, Mr. Secretary . . . I'm here. What? The President wants to invite His Royal Highness Prince Gow to Washington for a state visit! Well, sir, I

don't know how to tell you this ... The head of state of
Nonomura is now General Hung Kai. No, sir, he's not a
Communist. He's a defector. It will all be in my report
... He's our man all right ... He took over from our
man Colonel Num. Colonel Num? He took over from our
man Prince Gow. Perhaps the general could explain it
better to the Secretary of Defense.

PRINCE

Let me speak to him.

GENERAL

(Takes phone, stands at attention)

General Fitzhugh here ... Yes, sir ... The stuff? It's the
stuff Pakistan wouldn't take. I was going to let you know
where it was ... Well, it's not exactly in our hands ...
No, sir, it's not in Communist hands ... well, sir, it's in
the CIA's hands ... I was afraid you'd say that.

PRINCE

Let me speak to him.

GENERAL

(Covering phone)

The head of the CIA wants to talk to Buttermilk.

SAM

That's me.

(Grabs phone)

Hello, Happy Birthday. This is Buttermilk. Well, let me
put it simply. The marigolds are in bloom again. Sears
216

Roebuck delivered the plum pudding, which was hot and ready for eating. Hop-hop, said Alice to John . . . Yes, sir, thank you, sir. Mr. Ambassador, the President wants to speak to you.

RAYMOND

What President?

SAM

The President of the United States.

PRINCE

Oh, let me speak to Pat.

RAYMOND

Mr. President, Raymond Wilkins here. Yes, sir, yes, Mr. President, no, sir, yes, sir, I think I'd better start at the beginning. You see I had this Communist-CIA butler named Sam. Sam. S-A-M. Sam as in Uncle.

(*Sounds of planes*)

PRINCE

Let me speak to him.

(*Sounds of planes*)

SNELLING

Sounds like planes up there.

GENERAL

That can't be planes. I stopped those planes. I told them Plan B.

Counting Sheep

RAYMOND

Just a minute, Mr. President. Our planes have arrived.
I am sure that it will give you a thrill to hear them.

(Holds phone out)

PRINCE

Mr. President, this is Prince Gow. I just want to ask
you . . .

(Plane sound fades)

SNELLING

The planes are leaving.

GENERAL

Good.

PRINCE

(Shouts toward phone)

To get all these people out of my country.

RAYMOND

(Into phone)

Sorry, Mr. President, you want to know who's doing all
the shouting?

(Plane sound up)

SNELLING

They're coming back.

GENERAL

They can't be. I told them distinctly ...

(*Two bomb drops*)

SNELLING

My God, they're bombing the palace.

(*Sound effect of three bombs*)

GENERAL

That's Plan D. Bombing the palace is Plan D. I said on the phone Plan B.

(*Sound effect of three bombs*)

You heard me—what did I say?

RAYMOND

I heard you distinctly, General. You said Plan B.

(*Sound effect of two bombs*)

PRINCE

Is anybody there? Is anybody there?

(*Hangs up phone*)

Nobody's there.

(*Sound of bombs as*)

THE CURTAIN FALLS